JOHN McCAIN
AN AMERICAN HERO

John Perritano

STERLING CHILDREN'S BOOKS

New York

STERLING CHILDREN'S BOOKS
New York

An Imprint of Sterling Publishing Co., Inc.
1166 Avenue of the Americas
New York, NY 10036

ISBN 978-1-4549-3135-5

Distributed in Canada by Sterling Publishing
c/o Canadian Manda Group, 664 Annette Street
Toronto, Ontario, M6S 2C8, Canada
Distributed in the United Kingdom by GMC Distribution Services
Castle Place, 166 High Street, Lewes, East Sussex, BN7 1XU, England
Distributed in Australia by NewSouth Books, 45 Beach Street, Coogee, NSW 2034, Australia

For information about custom editions, special sales, and premium and corporate purchases,
please contact Sterling Special Sales at 800-805-5489 or specialsales@sterlingpublishing.com.

Manufactured in Canada
Lot #:
2 4 6 8 10 9 7 5 3 1
03/18

sterlingpublishing.com

Interior design by Alan Barnett Design/22MediaWorks
Cover design by Irene Vandervoort
Photo Credits appear on p. 185.

CONTENTS

Timeline

August 29, 1936	John Sidney McCain III is born at Coco Solo Naval Air Station, Panama Canal Zone.
1954	Graduates from Episcopal High School, Alexandria, Virginia.
1958	Graduates from the U.S. Naval Academy at Annapolis.
1960	Begins career as a naval aviator on the USS *Intrepid* and USS *Enterprise* in the Caribbean and Mediterranean Seas.
July 1967	Survives with injuries to his leg and chest when his A-4 Skyhawk is destroyed in a massive explosion and fire on the USS *Forrestal*.
October 1967	Taken prisoner by the North Vietnamese when his A-4E Skyhawk is shot down over Hanoi.
March 1973	Released by the North Vietnamese after five and a half years as a POW.
1981	Retires from the Navy with the rank of captain.
1982–1984	Elected to the U.S. House of Representatives and serves on the House Foreign Affairs Committee.
1986	Elected to the U.S. Senate. Re-elected in 1992, 1998, 2004 and 2010. Serves on the Armed Services Committee.
2000	Runs for the Republican Party nomination for president of the United States but loses to George W. Bush, who goes on to win the presidency.
2008	Becomes the Republican candidate for president of the United States but loses to Barack Obama.
2015	Becomes the chair of the Armed Services Committee.
2017	Diagnosed with terminal brain cancer.

INTRODUCTION

Profile in Courage

WHEN JOHN MCCAIN WAS 12 YEARS OLD, he discovered a four-leaf clover in a grassy patch. The boy was excited because he believed the discovery meant good luck. He placed the leaves in the first book he could snatch off his father's bookshelf. The book was Ernest Hemingway's *For Whom the Bell Tolls.*

After a time, McCain picked up the book, opened to the first chapter and began reading about its hero Robert Jordan, an American soldier fighting in the Spanish Civil War. Hemingway's heroic character resonated with young John. He wanted to emulate the kind of man Hemingway created. He was "the man I admired above almost all others in life and fiction," McCain writes in his book *Worth Fighting For: A Memoir.* "He was brave, dedicated, capable, selfless...a man who would risk his life but never his honor. He was and remains to my mind a hero..."

Over the years, John Sidney McCain III, the familiar white-haired senator from Arizona with a penchant for telling it like it is, has displayed steadfastness and courage, literally under fire, becoming a real-life Robert Jordan. "We often hear people now say, where are our heroes, where have all our heroes gone?" former U.S. Attorney General Griffin Bell once remarked. "Well, Senator McCain is an authentic, living American hero."

People have described John McCain in all kinds of ways—many positive, a few negative. Some say he is a fighter, a survivor, a hero, while others at times have called him difficult and mercurial. Regardless, John McCain holds a special place in our nation's history and in its heart. He is a Vietnam War veteran, shot down over enemy territory and captured. He survived nearly six years in a prisoner of war camp, where he was brutally beaten and tortured. He lived through plane crashes, survived a fire aboard an aircraft carrier, and thrived in a decades-long political career. He endured two failed presidential runs, but never became bitter.

While McCain served gallantly in war, it was during his political life that he would accomplish what was most important to him—serving the American people. In the political arena, McCain has been touted by friend and foe as a maverick, a person who did not bend with the political winds, but stood up for his ideals no matter the consequences. McCain earned a reputation for independence and took stands on issues that irritated his fellow Republicans, including several presidents.

Yet, as Robert Timberg writes in *John McCain: An American Odyssey*, the term "maverick" can be "a two-edged sword in that it may trivialize [the time] he has spent in Congress as a hardworking, effective legislator."

John McCain is more complicated than any label suggests. During four years in the House of Representatives and more than two decades in the Senate, he defined himself as a mainstream conservative who was willing to compromise on many issues for the good of the nation.

Growing up John McCain was not easy. Perhaps it is because he carried the weight of family tradition on his shoulders. He grew up in a family whose service to country came before anything else. His grandfather was a naval aviator, his father a submariner. Both were respected, outsized men in their own right. They had fought battles and helped win wars. Both ascended to the highest rank in the U.S. Navy. They were John McCain's first heroes, eclipsing even the fictional Robert Jordan. Earning their respect was the light that guided McCain throughout his life.

Such shoes are tough to fill, especially when a person is *expected* to fill them. While most people don't have their lives planned out for them, John McCain was an exception. His grandfather and father *expected* John McCain to be a sailor just as they were. They *expected* him to attend the

Senator John McCain is often called a true American hero.

U.S. Naval Academy, just as they did. They *expected* that if he was called to serve in combat, he would do so with loyalty, bravery and integrity, just as they had.

With such pressure, it is no wonder that John McCain III took pleasure in being irreverent and rowdy. As a youngster, he flouted rules and refused to adapt to the normal constraints of authority. McCain had a temper and lived for a time, by his own admission, an indulgent life.

Ironically, the brashness forged as a child and as a young man is what might have saved his life in the enemy's prisons. He endured more pain and anguish than a person should ever expect to suffer in one lifetime. He did his family proud. He did his nation proud.

Senators John McCain and Barack Obama shake hands before a debate in 2007.

"I have spent much of my life choosing my own attitude, often carelessly, often for no better reason than to indulge conceit," McCain writes. "In those instances, my acts of self-determination were mistakes, some of which did no lasting harm…Others I deeply regret.

"At other times, I choose my own way with good cause and to good effect. I did not do so to apologize for my mistakes…When I chose well I did so to keep a balance in my life—a balance between pride and regret, between liberty and honor."

McCain's path was not easy. He attended 20 different schools and was married twice. He had flaws, McCain readily notes, for he was human. "I am older than dirt and have more scars than Frankenstein," he often said. Yet he had a heart as big as an aircraft carrier and cared about how government treated people.

"I learned long ago that serving only oneself is petty and unsatisfying ambition," he told his supporters after winning the New Hampshire Republican primary for president on January 8, 2008. "But serve a cause greater than self-interest and you will know happiness far more sublime than the fleeting pleasure of fame and fortune. For me that greater cause has always been my country, which I have served imperfectly for many years, but have loved without any reservation every day of my life."

John McCain is a true American and a man who has influenced the lives of people all over the world.

CHAPTER 1

A Naval Family

John McCain III was born on August 29, 1936, the son and grandson of U.S. Navy career officers. His father and grandfather loved both the Navy and their country. McCain was a Navy brat who came into this world on a remote naval base in Panama where his father was stationed. It was one of many military bases that McCain would see as a child, teenager and adult.

Growing up a child in the military is often difficult. Kids are bounced from one place to the next. They usually don't spend enough time in one location to make good friends or put down roots in a community. To make matters worse, the child of a soldier, sailor or airman has to endure the absence of a parent for long stretches. It can be a lonely life.

Yet there is something that a child of the military learns quickly— the ability, in McCain's words, "to think of the country as greater than ourselves, to love it not exclusively but wholeheartedly. Even if we don't heed the lessons at first, war will usually convert us. And it becomes a love we cannot part with."

As a teenager, McCain did not talk openly about whether he wanted to follow in his father's and grandfather's footsteps. But he did have seawater in his veins. McCain admired both men, but it was his grandfather, John Sidney McCain Sr., nicknamed "Slew," who would hold a special place in his heart. When the admiral walked by, McCain would proudly point and tell his friends, "That's my grandfather, right there."

John S. McCain III sits between his grandfather, John Sidney "Slew" McCain Sr., and his father, John Sidney McCain Jr., in a family photo from the 1940s.

Slew McCain

"Slew" McCain was a diehard Navy man. He was thin with a hooked nose and sunken cheeks.

"My grandfather loved his children," McCain writes in his memoir, *Faith of My Fathers*. "And my father admired my grandfather above all others. My mother, to whom my father was devoted, had once asked him if he loved his father more than he loved her. He replied simply, 'Yes, I do.'"

Although Slew McCain would achieve high military rank, he was a second-rate student at the U.S. Naval Academy. It was something he would have in common with his son and grandson. Sometimes, though, a person doesn't have to be at the top of the class to make an impact. Within a decade or so after graduation, Slew outpaced all his classmates. He became one of the first naval aviators in the United States. He later achieved the exalted rank of vice admiral. For six months in 1942, Slew McCain commanded all naval aircraft in the South Pacific.

He was crusty, decisive, ornery. *Collier's* magazine put him on the cover of its October 23, 1942, issue titled "Navy Air Boss." "In today's slang," his grandson writes, "he lived large…he liked to take his shoes off when he worked and walk around the office in his stocking feet."

When World War II began for the United States in 1941, Slew McCain was sixty years old. He looked much older. His dentures didn't fit. He spoke with a slight whistle. He fidgeted and was high-strung, all traits he would pass on to his grandson.

"There were few wiser or more competent officers in the Navy than Slew," wrote historian E.B. Potter, "but whenever his name came up, somebody had a ridiculous story to tell about him—and many of the stories were true." Like the time on Guadalcanal, an island in the Pacific, which the United States had just taken from the Japanese, its enemy in the region. Vice Admiral McCain was inspecting the embattled island with two other naval commanders. Although the Japanese had been beaten, their planes still bombed the atoll regularly. One night as the dignitaries slept in a hut, an enemy aircraft passed overhead. The men could hear its engines rattle the night sky. The air raid siren blew its ominous warning. Slew McCain bounded from the hut. As bombs dropped, he ran half-naked into a warm hole full of foul water from a latrine.

In the final months of the war, Slew McCain commanded one of Admiral William "Bull" Halsey's aircraft carrier task forces. During the war, carrier groups were formidable weapons. They consisted of an aircraft carrier accompanied by a number of ships and attack planes. With his armada, Slew unleashed an unbearable fury on the Japanese fleet. He was also on the deck of the USS *Missouri* when the Japanese surrendered to the Allied forces, led by the United States, Great Britain, France and the Soviet Union. Slew was full of pride as he stood among the throng of servicemen that had assembled on the ship.

John Sidney "Slew" McCain

Four days later, Slew arrived back home to his wife in California.

On the fifth day after that homecoming, John McCain's grandmother, Katherine Vaulx McCain, threw her husband a welcome-home celebration. Friends, family and neighbors attended. At the party were the families of Navy friends who had yet to return from the war.

As he stood in the crowded living room, people peppered Slew with questions. They wanted to know what it was like to be on the deck of the *Missouri* when the enemy surrendered. The wives of men who had been prisoners of war wanted any tidbit of information about their husbands. Were they safe? When might they come home? Slew McCain answered each as best as he could. Then he turned to his wife and told her he wasn't feeling well. McCain then collapsed. A doctor who was at the party checked his pulse. "Kate, he's dead," the physician said.

John "Slew" McCain was gone. He was 61 years old. He died of a heart attack, brought on, some speculated, by the furious fighting in the Pacific during the last months of the war. In other words, Slew McCain was one of the war's last casualties. Some believed he had had an earlier heart attack at sea, but kept it hidden.

"I knew him as well as anybody in the world, with the possible exception of my mother," John McCain's father later said, describing the last conversation he had with his dad. "He looked in fine health to me, and God knows his conversation was anything but indicative of a man who was sick. And two days later he died of a heart attack."

John Sidney McCain's death was on the front page of the *New York Times*. "Admiral McCain's groups were called the world's most powerful task force and the destruction they wrought upon Japanese military installations … and centers played a vital role in reducing the country's ability to fight and bringing about final victory," the obituary read.

Five years later, Slew McCain made headlines once again. It was a small story tucked into the back pages of the *New York Times*: "McCain Promotion." The story began: "President Truman signed today a bill giving a posthumous promotion to Vice Admiral John S. McCain. The bill directs the Navy to change its records to show that Admiral McCain received the rank of admiral as of Sept. 6, 1945, the date of his death. The promotion is an honorary one.… He commanded Task Force 38 in the Pacific during the war."

★ ★ ★ ★ ★ ★ ★ ★ ★ ★ ★ ★ ★ ★ ★ ★

The U.S. Navy in 1936

When John McCain was born in 1936, the U.S. Navy was a much different place than it is today. Promotions were handed out sparingly. Although the Navy had almost 500,000 sailors, officers were scarce. They were a tight-knit group.

When John's parents, Jack and Roberta, were stationed in Hawaii, the men would join their wives for dinner wearing starched white uniforms with black ties. By the 1930s, the Navy was modernizing, building aircraft carriers capable of launching planes from the middle of the ocean. Aboard the aircraft carrier is where John McCain would find his calling.

A Sailor in Iowa?

John McCain's father, John Sidney McCain Jr., a seaman like his dad, had been born in the middle of the Corn Belt, far from the ocean. It just so happened that a very pregnant Katherine McCain was visiting relatives in Iowa while her husband was at sea. It was there she gave birth to John McCain's father.

John Jr. grew up understanding the particulars of life in a military family. The separations. The constant moving. Life always shuffled like a deck of cards. He also knew what was expected of him. He was the son of one of the Navy's most important officers. It was a lot to live up to, a ton of weight on his young shoulders. Like his father, Slew, a Navy officer is what John McCain Jr. would become.

John Jr. was a thin, slight 16-year-old, standing 5 feet 6 inches tall and weighing a mere 133 pounds, when his father dropped him off at the U.S. Naval Academy in Annapolis, Maryland. By most measures he was much too young for the challenges he would face.

From the beginning, it seemed as if John Jr. had something to prove. Students at the Naval Academy were called midshipmen. First-year students were called plebes. In social standing, plebes were the lowest rung of the ladder, the dirt on the bottom of the upperclassmen's shoes. Plebes were required to answer to the upperclassmen, bow to their every wish, obey every command. The instructors were tough. The assignments were brain-busting. The physical exertion was beyond anything John Jr. had ever experienced before.

Perhaps it was because he wasn't as tall or as weighty as the other midshipmen that John Jr. found ways around the academy's rules. He defied authority and battled those who picked on him. "He would fight at the drop of a hat," his son writes. His grades weren't good, yet he was able to weather the grueling workload while other midshipmen faltered. Some of those students dropped out. Others were expelled. But John McCain Jr. had his dad's stubbornness and grit. He survived the U.S. Naval Academy— but barely. A record of his first term shows 114 infractions, for which he received demerits. Demerits are handed out by the Navy for bad behavior, including lying, cheating, stealing and drinking alcohol. During the second term McCain received 219 demerits.

Such conduct was not becoming a midshipman. John Jr.'s superiors at the academy warned him several times with letters that read: "The Superintendent notes with concern that you are unsatisfactory in your Academic work…and he wishes to take this opportunity to point out that unless you devote your entire effort to improve your scholastic work you are in grave danger of being found deficient at the end of the year."

Copies of those letters went to his parents.

Nevertheless, John Jr. made it through, thanks, in part, to two roommates. They were beefy linemen on the varsity football team. Looking on the vice admiral's son as a little brother, they took John Jr. under their wing, helping him through the hazing of his first year and even taking the blame when he screwed up.

Eventually, John Jr. graduated and began his career in the Navy, a job that he loved perhaps more than anything in the world. For John Jr. the Navy came first. He was a seaman, just like his father. All his thoughts were given over, in some fashion, to the Navy. He read books related to naval history, strategy, and tactics. And with the exception of tennis, he wasn't much interested in sports or hunting or fishing. John Jr. married Roberta Wright in 1933. The two met when she was a student at the University of California. They eloped and married in the Mexican border town of Tijuana in a place called Caesar's Bar. In 1934, he received orders to go to Hawaii and serve as an ensign on a submarine. His wife was eagerly awaiting the trip to what she called "paradise."

"The Navy revered my father's and grandfather's shared ideals and offered them adventure," John Jr.'s son would later write. "It promised them the perfect life, and they were grateful to their last breath for the privilege."

In Hawaii, John Jr. worked long hours when he wasn't away at sea. He worked hard to please his superiors. He did not turn down any assignment. He wanted to move up the ladder of command. "No matter what job you get," he told his wife, "you can make a good one out of it."

John Jr. moved up the ranks. In June 1943, a year and a half after the United States entered World War II, John Jr. was a lieutenant commander aboard the submarine *Gunnel*, which at that time was tasked with patrolling the waters between Midway Island and the Japanese city of Nagasaki. One day his crew caught sight of seven large Japanese freighters and two smaller ships heading for Shanghai. The convoy was moving fast. Much too fast for the *Gunnel*, which was following underwater. A submarine cannot move fast when it is submerged. At the speed the *Gunnel* was going, the convoy would be long gone before the sub had a chance to attack.

A McCain family picture taken around 1944.

Knowing this, and knowing the dangers of riding on the surface (a submarine is, literally, a sitting duck when riding on top of the water), John Jr. gave the order to surface. In moments, the *Gunnel*'s speed nearly doubled. As the hours ticked by, the *Gunnel* raced to cut off the Japanese convoy.

Finally, at 5:30 a.m. on June 19, the *Gunnel* had moved close enough to engage the enemy. When the first ship was in the *Gunnel's* sites, John Jr. gave the order to fire. A torpedo swam from the *Gunnel*, hitting its mark, exploding and sinking a freighter. The *Gunnel* fired at another ship, sinking it.

Then John Jr. ordered the submarine to dive. The Japanese counterattacked by launching depth charges, bombs that explode underneath the surface. The explosions rattled the sub. Sailors who have been in similar circumstances described it as if they were inside a steel tube while someone was hitting it with a sledgehammer.

Once again John Jr. made a command decision. He gave the order to surface. If he and his crew were going to die, they would die with honor, defending their lives and their country. The *Gunnel* fought back, sinking another ship. Then John Jr. ordered the submarine to dive once again. And there it sat, under the water, for 36 hours.

The air inside the sub became unbearably hot. It was hard to breathe. The *Gunnel* crew struggled for each gulp of precious oxygen. Finally, the *Gunnel* had to surface, not only to take in fresh air, but to recharge its batteries. As the sub surfaced, John Jr. and the crew looked for any sign of the remaining Japanese ships. Luckily, they had left the area. The *Gunnel* and its crew motored back to port victorious—and, more importantly, alive. The Navy awarded John Jr. a Silver Star for "conspicuous gallantry and intrepidity in action, as Commanding Officer of a submarine in enemy Japanese-controlled waters…[and] bravery under fire and aggressive fighting spirit."

It would be that same courageous spirit that would keep his son alive in the darkest hours of desperation.

CHAPTER 2

Early Life

THE COCO SOLO NAVAL AIR STATION DOESN'T EXIST ANYMORE. The base, on the Atlantic side of the Panama Canal, was shut down by the U.S. Department of Defense in 1999. In 1936, however, Coco Solo was an important part of the region's defense system. The United States had built the base in 1918, four years after workers finished the Panama Canal, the main thoroughfare for sea-going vessels crossing between the Atlantic and Pacific oceans.

Cutting across the isthmus of Panama, a curved ribbon of land in Central America, the 50-mile canal was the most strategic spot in the Western Hemisphere. In the past, American naval vessels sailed around the tip of South America—a dangerous and long voyage—to move between the two oceans. The canal provided a shortcut. It had to be protected. That was the job of those stationed at Coco Solo.

Slew McCain was the commander of the base. His son, John Jr., was stationed nearby at a small submarine facility. When John (Johnny) McCain III was born on August 29, 1936, it was one of the few times all three generations of McCains were in the same place at the same time.

McCain was born on a Saturday at around 11 a.m. His mother, Roberta, remembered decades later, "The hospital was close to the officers' club and...all these men gathered at this club to celebrate this child's arrival."

Two months after his birth, John McCain, wrapped in baby clothes and held in his mother's arms, was on the move for the first time in his life. The Navy had transferred his father to a submarine base in New London, Connecticut.

★ ★ ★ ★ ★ ★ ★ ★ ★ ★ ★ ★ ★ ★ ★ ★

Coco Solo Controversy

The place where John McCain was born might not have seemed significant in 1936. But 72 years later, when he ran for president of the United States, critics claimed that McCain was not a "natural born citizen," one of the constitutional requirements for becoming president. His detractors claimed, correctly, that McCain was not born at the air base because Coco Solo did not have a hospital until 1941. However, McCain was born at the submarine base's small hospital. Moreover, McCain argued that he was a U.S. citizen because both his parents were U.S. citizens. In addition, the Panama Canal Zone was effectively under U.S. control. The matter was quickly closed and no one mentioned it again.

John's Mother, Roberta

As a young child, John McCain did not want for anything. Although the salary of a naval officer was paltry, McCain's mother was from a wealthy family. Her father had made his fortune when he struck oil in the Southwestern United States. He made so much money that he retired at the very young age of 40 shortly after Roberta McCain and her identical twin sister, Rowena, were born. "I've just had two daughters, and I'm going to stay home and enjoy my family," their father said, as quoted in *John McCain: An American Odyssey*, by Robert Timberg.

Roberta's father kept true to his word. He took his daughters to school and the theater and made sure they went to dance class. As the years passed, many people had trouble telling the beautiful sisters apart.

If John McCain inherited any trait from his mother, it was her resilience and spirit. Her can-do attitude and ability to rise to any challenge helped the family through many trying moments, especially during World War II. McCain's family included an older sister, Sandy, and a younger brother, Joe. With their dad gone most of the time, Roberta was the commander in chief of the McCain household. She did the grunt work, dressing

McCain Field at the U.S. Navy training base in Meridian, Mississippi, was named in honor of Admiral John S. McCain Sr. in 1961.

her children, wiping their tears, nursing them through sicknesses and sadness, and scolding them when needed. She picked the schools her children attended. She made sure their homework was done. Roberta also found and purchased the family's homes. She had an impetuous nature, something her son, John, would inherit. She once bought a brand-new car when she was supposed to be shopping for a new dress. When she paid bills with a check, she signed her husband's name in her own handwriting. When John Jr. tried to pay a bill, the check often came back marked as a forgery. The signatures didn't match.

A Brat in All Ways

John McCain III developed a bad temper as he grew up. He was a Navy brat, of course, the term used to describe children of career military personnel. But he also behaved like a brat! "At the smallest provocation, I would go off in a mad frenzy, and then, suddenly crash to the floor unconscious," McCain remembers. John Jr. and Roberta became so concerned about this bizarre behavior that they took their son to a Navy doctor.

The doctor examined the boy and shook his head. Not to worry, he said. John was fine. He was simply being a little terror. When the boy became angry, the doctor said, he held his breath until he passed out. The doctor then prescribed a treatment that, McCain later wrote, would seem harsh by today's standards. Yet it was effective. He told John Jr. and Roberta to fill a bathtub with cold water when John acted up. If he began to hold his breath, the doctor instructed, they should submerge the child in the tub of water, clothes and all.

"I do not recall at all these traumatic early encounters with the harsh consequences of my misbehavior, buried, as they must be, deep in my subconscious," McCain writes in his autobiography. "But my mother assures me that they occurred, and went on some time until I was finally 'cured.' Whenever I worked myself into a tiny rage, my mother shouted to my father, 'Get the water!' Moments later I would find myself thrashing wide-eyed and gasping for breath, in a tub of icy-cold water."

Eventually, John learned how to control his outrageous behavior. Moreover, the cold-water cure instilled in him a need for what he described as "equal justice under the law."

"After my first few experiences with the dreaded immersion therapy, I would shout 'Get the water! Get the water!' whenever my older sister, Sandy, momentarily lost control of her temper."

Second-Rate Education

Because the McCain family moved so often, it was hard for John and his siblings to get a decent education. Schools on military bases were notoriously found lacking in the quality of education they provided. Schools were usually housed in an old aircraft hangar. Students of different ages were thrown into one class. The teacher the students had on a Monday might not be the one who showed up on Tuesday, Wednesday or Friday.

When the Navy transferred John Jr. and his family to Long Beach, California, they were horrified by the state of the base school. John Jr. was incensed at the lack of educational opportunities the Navy provided for his children. In desperation, he visited the rectory of a Catholic church. Though the McCains were Episcopalian, he pleaded with the monsignor, the head of the parish, to allow his children to attend the parish school. John Jr. offered to have his family convert to Catholicism if that is what the monsignor wished. The priest stopped McCain's father with a wave of his hand. That wouldn't be necessary, the monsignor said. He'd admit the McCain children to the school regardless of their religion.

While McCain's parents hated how their child's education was progressing in the navy schools, John actually loved it. It was informal and at times fun. Even after the children began attending parochial school, Roberta took on the added responsibility of furthering their education. McCain called her "an imaginative and amusing educator."

The future Senator McCain with his sister, Sandy, in 1938.

"Like wealthy parents who 'finish' their children's education with a tour of the European continent, my mother saw our frequent cross-country trips to join my father as an opportunity to supplement our irregular schooling," McCain writes. "She was forever routing our journeys through locations that offered a site of historical significance or a notable institute of arts or sciences."

It was, at times, an amazing journey. Art galleries. Museums. Churches. Geological wonders. Civil War battlefields. Monuments to American heroes. All of these became John McCain's classrooms. As he got older, he remembered each with gratitude and excitement. His mother was always the tour guide.

Still, John McCain was not the best student. When he was around 12, John Jr. and Roberta enrolled their son at the private St. Stephen's School in Washington, D.C., after the family had relocated there. The school was exclusive and expectations were high. John, however, disappointed greatly. His unruliness reached new heights. The faculty was aghast at the boy's terrible behavior. It was only the beginning.

Family Traits

Although they were often at odds, John and his mother, Roberta, were similar in character. John emulated many of his mother's traits, often to the point of exaggeration. Roberta oozed charm and graciousness. She was talkative. John was even more so, to the point of being boisterous. Roberta was enthusiastic. John became unruly.

Still, Roberta passed on many outstanding qualities. She taught John to find the pleasure in life even in the presence of misfortune. She taught him to show strength in the face of adversity. It was a lesson he took to heart. Even in his darkest moments, John McCain never surrendered.

While John was rowdy and unruly, his father had a more moderate temper and stayed mostly silent. "My father was often quiet at the dinner table," brother Joe said; "the rest of us raised hell, argued, until Dad would intervene—always on my mother's behalf. John was either fiercely immersed in the squabble or the root cause of it."

McCain's father had barely survived the Naval Academy, but he was an intelligent man. He even taught electrical engineering from 1938 to 1940. Most students thought he was a good instructor. John Jr. was also a lover of history and English literature. He could recite poems committed to memory.

His son loved literature, too. John McCain discovered his love of books at the age of 10 when he visited his paternal grandmother in Coronado, California. In between the maid summoning him to tea and supper every day, McCain read books that his father had kept as a child. The authors included Mark Twain, Robert Louis Stevenson and James Fenimore Cooper. "These works instilled in me a lifelong love of reading," McCain said. "And, with their straightforward moral lessons, they reinforced my sense of right and wrong and impressed upon me the virtue of treating people fairly."

There is no doubt that John McCain loved and respected his father. Yet, while he often wrote in glowing terms about his mother's personality and their loving relationship, McCain's views about his father, at least on paper, centered around his intelligence, his mastery of naval strategy, his achievements, and his sense of loyalty, honor and duty. He tried to make sense of his father's state of mind, writing that his dad had an "oppressive desire to honor his father's name."

"I hesitate to write that my father was insecure, but he was thrust into difficult circumstances at such a young age that it would have been very hard to resist self-doubts," McCain writes. "He was an aspiring man whose ambition to meet the standard of his famous father might have collided with his appreciation for the implausibility of the accomplishment. Nevertheless, he would succeed, and become the Navy's first son of a four-star admiral to reach the same rank as his father…

"When I was young, similarities between my mother and me were more apparent than were those between my father and me. My father and I probably seemed in many respects…very different people."

While hugs and kisses might have been in short supply, John Jr. had a profound impact on his son's life. It was John Jr. (along with his grandfather) who instilled in John McCain ideals of service, loyalty and love of country, and, above all, a call to duty. All those traits, coupled with his mother's determined spirit, served McCain well later in life.

Episcopal High School

Throughout his young life, John McCain had a hard time forming lasting friendships. He attended 20 different schools. He was also a small child who would quickly prove to new schoolmates that he was not to be messed with. The fastest way to instill such a lesson, at least in young McCain's mind, was to fight the first kid who aggravated him. Whether he won or lost the fight wasn't the point. Gaining respect was. "I foolishly believed that fighting, as well as challenging school authorities and ignoring school regulations, was indispensable to my self-esteem and helped me to form new friendships."

The future senator in a photograph from his senior year in high school.

Just the opposite happened. McCain had few friends to speak of. He knew some of this isolation was because he was the son of a serviceman. He expected it. So, between the fighting and the moving from place to place, the friendships he did have were intense, but did not last long.

The situation changed once his parents enrolled him in Episcopal High School in Alexandria, Virginia, in 1951. The school left a major impression on McCain. The all-white, all-male student body consisted of children from rich Southern families. Fathers, grandfathers and great-grandfathers had attended the school. That made McCain, the son of a sailor, somewhat of an outcast. The only discussions surrounding the military were stories about heroes of the Confederacy.

McCain learned that many of those who attended Episcopal had their lives already mapped out. They would graduate, enroll in the University of Virginia, or an Ivy League school like Yale, Princeton or Harvard, then go to work in the family business. McCain, in a way, had more in common with them than he might have realized. His destiny had been written two generations before. Episcopal was the last stop before his appointment to the U.S. Naval Academy. Once he graduated he would enter the U.S. Navy—the McCain family business.

Episcopal High School proved challenging. Students were expected to follow the rigorous traditions and teachings of the Episcopal Church in both their academic pursuits and their behavior. As always, McCain rebelled. He was high-spirited and combative. A friend would later say he had been a "punk." His nickname was "Nasty."

The school had a dress code. McCain, of course, ignored it. He wore blue jeans and other ratty outfits. His shoes were held together with tape.

"John used to wear his jeans day in, and day out, week in, week out, to where they would almost stand up in the corner by themselves," one friend related to historian Robert Timberg. "And a lot of people thought he maybe should have washed a little more or something. His blue jeans would be just filthy."

McCain entered Episcopal High School as a sophomore. Yet, like his father before him, he still had to deal with hazing upperclassmen who humiliated and degraded new or younger students. Episcopal High's newbies were called Rats. When McCain arrived, he was considered the Worst Rat. Nothing he did pleased the upperclassmen. McCain didn't care. He was proud to be Episcopal High's Worst Rat. He was tough. He was mean. "He was seemingly ready to fight at the drop of a hat," a friend told Timberg.

McCain, center, channeled some of his aggression into sports. He was a fiercely competitive member of Episcopal High School's wrestling team.

Eventually McCain straightened out and learned to work within the boundaries of his high school, rather than against it. As an adult he came to understand how hard the staff worked to instill a sense of order and duty in the often unruly students. Speaking about his high school experience, in 1999 McCain remarked, "I'm a victim of Episcopal High School. The principles embodied in the school, and especially the honor code, are those I've tried to embody in my own life. I haven't always succeeded… but I've tried."

CHAPTER 3

The Naval Academy

MORE THAN ANYTHING, John McCain approached his education with indifference. He liked English and history and usually did well in those classes. Yet he didn't stand out at Episcopal High.

Still, a few months before graduation, McCain signed up for a course that would help him with the entrance exam to the U.S. Naval Academy. Uncharacteristically, he applied himself and did well on the test. It was a big achievement for him and increased his confidence in his abilities. McCain no longer doubted he would follow in his father's and grandfather's footsteps.

On June 28, 1954, John Jr. drove his son to the Naval Academy after vacationing in Virginia Beach. "In those days an officer escorting his son to the Naval Academy was thought to be an event charged with symbolic importance...I don't remember it so," McCain writes. "I had long expected the day, so often envisioned the drive, that the actual event seemed more familiar than remarkable. I remember being nervous, and my father offering me typical words of encouragement. But nothing occurred in that one-hour trip that affected my long-held paradoxical image of the Academy, a place that I belonged at but dreaded."

Plebe Year

John McCain arrived at Annapolis with the weight of his seafaring family firmly planted on his shoulders. Along with his classmates, now known as midshipmen, he raised his right hand, swore an oath and began his march toward an uncertain future. Yet he knew something most of the other midshipmen did not know. The academy was not the real Navy. He knew from his grandfather and his father how the "real Navy" worked. The academy was on a lofty pedestal, where officers learned how to comport themselves at tea parties and cocktail receptions at the club. Still, when the bullets and shells started flying, Naval Academy grads could die just as easily as a lowly seaman. It was a weighty understanding for an 18-year-old on his way to becoming a naval officer.

First up for the young men of the class of '58 was to learn a whole new vocabulary. Floors became "decks." Walls were "bulkheads." The restrooms were "lavatories."

McCain and all the other midshipmen had to abide by the Honor Code. The slightest departure from its rigorous expectations meant expulsion, ridicule and dishonor. It read:

> *Midshipmen are persons of integrity: They stand for that which is right. They tell the truth and ensure that the truth is known. They do not lie. They embrace fairness in all actions. They ensure that work submitted as their own is their own, and that assistance received from a source is authorized and properly documented. They do not cheat. They respect the property of others and ensure that others are able to benefit from the use of their own property. They do not steal.*

John McCain dressed in the uniform of a naval aviator.

Once again, McCain was subjected to the hazing system. The upperclassmen ruled over the plebes like despotic monarchs. Each plebe was required to read a small handbook called *Reef Points* and memorize it, chapter and verse. If an upperclassman asked a plebe to recite from the so-called midshipman's bible, the plebe had to answer correctly or face the consequences, which could include walking around on all fours like a dog for most of the day.

Some might say that McCain's background gave him some status on campus. His father was a Navy captain. Captains commanded aircraft carriers, submarines and battleships. It is more than likely, however, that McCain's father's rank did not win his son any special treatment. It would not save McCain's brother, Joe, from failure a few years later. In 1961, Joe would "wash out," or "bilge out," of the academy. Johnny was not about to squander his chances. If he kept his temper in check and his shenanigans to a hair-raising minimum, he could get through just about any situation.

Yet the Naval Academy was not an easy place to live or to study. For centuries midshipmen talked about the academy in scary ways. Some described it as a place where a person's basic rights were taken away, only to be given back one by one. It was rough for the toughest of young men, and "just getting by" was unacceptable.

But Annapolis was also a place of tradition, and many great sailors, some of whom won the Congressional Medal of Honor—the highest achievement for valor in the U.S. military—had attended school there. The academy's job was to mold future leaders, and nothing was more important in that process than plebe year. The purpose of plebe year was to separate the weak freshmen who could not stand up to the discipline and rigors of Navy life from the ones who were able. The process was brutal, but the system required it. There was a method to all the madness and abuse. The rules and hazing were used to tcst a person's endurance. Plebe year was designed to build respect, character and honor. As Timberg writes, superiors gave the plebes more than they could handle just to see how much they *could* handle.

Some good men quit. Almost everyone thought about leaving at some point. Duty, honor, country. They were the three words branded on the mind of each plebe.

★ ★ ★ ★ ★ ★ ★ ★ ★ ★ ★ ★ ★ ★ ★

Qualifications of a Naval Officer

John Paul Jones was one of the greatest naval commanders in U.S. history. Born in Scotland in 1742, he first went to sea when he was 13 years old, and by 21 he was a ship's captain. During the American Revolution, a British commander asked Jones whether he wished to surrender his ship during a battle. "I have not begun to fight," was the seaman's answer.

In *Reef Points*, there is a passage from Jones relating to the qualifications of a naval officer. "It is by no means enough that an officer of the Navy should be a capable mariner. He must be that, of course, but also a great deal more. He should be as well a gentleman of liberal education, refined manners… courtesy…and personal honor…. In one word, every commander should keep constantly before him the great truth, that is to be well obeyed, he must be perfectly esteemed."

Caste System

An hour after arriving at the academy, McCain went to the barber and had his head shaved. The transition from civilian life to military life was immediate. Seniors were called first classmen or "firsties." Juniors were second classmen, or segundos; sophomores were third classmen, or youngsters. And freshmen were fourth classmen, or, of course, plebes.

"To my surprise, I liked it at first," McCain writes of "plebe summer," the point in the year when the freshmen have the academy all to themselves before the arrival of the upperclassmen. He wrestled, boxed and ran the obstacle course. Although he wasn't interested in academics, McCain was quick-witted and crafty. He even embraced the military lifestyle to a point, learning to march in formation. He caught the eyes of his superiors who thought that McCain had what it took to be a class leader. They even appointed him a company commander. Annapolis had started out well for the young John McCain.

"I had good grease, which meant I showed a natural aptitude for the service and possessed…leadership qualities.… I liked almost every minute of it until the time when my education at the Naval Academy began in earnest. I liked it until plebe summer concluded with the return of the upperclassmen from their vacations, eager to commence their campaign to humiliate, degrade, and make miserable me and every other plebe they encountered."

Not much had changed at Annapolis since the days of Slew McCain and John Jr. If an upperclassman walked by, McCain was expected to sit up or stand up straight, chin tucked into his neck. Each day he and the other plebes were expected to conduct meaningless tasks. If an upperclassman asked a question, no matter how stupid or obscure, the freshmen were obligated to find the answer.

Yes, sir. No, sir. Aye, aye, sir. I'll find out, sir. These were the words that McCain uttered every day to men who he thought did not deserve his respect. If a plebe such as McCain could endure the hardships handed out by the upperclassmen, then he was just as good as they were—if not better.

Shoes had to gleam. Brass buckles had to shine. Collars had to be stiff. Shirts had to be tucked in correctly. McCain failed this part of his training at every turn. He was as slovenly as a midshipman could be, reminiscent of his blatant disregard of the Episcopal High School dress code. He crammed for tests with the help of his friends. He didn't spend a lot of time on subjects that he didn't like. He wanted to know just enough to get by.

Robert Timberg has observed that, "Rebellious by nature, [McCain] viewed rules and regulations through a highly personal prism, as challenges to his wit and ingenuity. And as a succession of individuals and institutions would learn—among them his parents, teachers, Annapolis officialdom, and [later] his jailers in Hanoi—all bets were off when Johnny McCain thought the rules were unfair, stupid, or as most were in his estimation, made to be broken."

It wasn't long before the "grease" he had accumulated started to rub off and the real John McCain began to emerge. "For a short time in my last year at the Academy, I would again possess good grease. But that was to be an anomaly in a long history of transgressions and improprieties."

Yet McCain kept his experiences during plebe year in perspective. His father, who was only 16 when he arrived at Annapolis, had to endure worse. John Jr. had been cruelly hazed. But his father was up to the task and proved himself an equal to any one at the academy.

McCain was not about to fall short.

★ ★ ★ ★ ★ ★ ★ ★ ★ ★ ★ ★ ★ ★ ★

The Naval Academy at a Glance

The U.S. Naval Academy began as the Naval School on October 10, 1845. At that time, Secretary of the Navy George Bancroft established the school without any money from Congress. The school was founded on a 10-acre Army post named Fort Severn in Annapolis, Maryland. The first class consisted of 50 midshipmen and seven professors. The students studied mathematics, navigation, gunnery, chemistry, natural philosophy, English and French.

Five years later, the school became the U.S. Naval Academy. The courses changed and each midshipman had to study for four years and train aboard ships each summer. The academy expanded as the U.S. Navy did. The campus ballooned to 338 acres. The number of students rose from 50 midshipmen to 4,000.

McCain refused to be beat, but he knew he had to control his temper. So he took the hazing. He endured the slights. He ignored the insults. He complied, but grudgingly. He did so not as a sign of respect for the upperclassmen, but as a sign of respect for himself.

"I did not accept that the abuse they had suffered in their plebe year now gave them the moral authority to abuse me. The Academy granted them that authority, and I wanted to remain at the Academy. I did not want to break. So I suffered the tyranny to the extent necessary to avoid bilging (washing) out. But no more than that…I hoped that was something in my manner that gave the impression that I lacked proper enthusiasm for the task."

Madcap McCain

At Annapolis, John McCain was an enemy of the system. Yet he was no longer the "punk" from Episcopal High. Instead, McCain became a leader, albeit a mischievous one. He was one of the most popular midshipmen in his class. His personality attracted many of his classmates to him. They responded to his charisma and his charm. They wanted McCain to like them.

He wasn't the tallest or the strongest. But he was the toughest. He was the leader of the Bad Bunch, a group of midshipmen who flouted authority and often paid the price.

"Our exploits were well known to most midshipmen, as well as to Academy authorities," McCain writes. "We were hardly as daring as we regarded ourselves, but we managed to defy most of the rules without committing any breach of the honor code. We were in search of a good time, which led us over the Academy walls on many an evening."

One night, McCain led his gang to a local saloon just outside Annapolis. It was a small, dirty place with sawdust on the floor and a shuffleboard machine in the corner. Midshipmen could leave the academy and go to a bar only if it was no more than seven miles away. This particular watering hole was off limits. It was eight miles from campus.

No matter—McCain and the Bad Bunch marched into this ramshackle dive as if they were kings of the world.

As the midshipmen hung out, the Shore Patrol, the Navy's police force, burst through the door. "No one move," one of the officers shouted. Of course, everyone did, each trying to make his escape. Some hid nearby in boats. Others broke through wire-mesh screens. McCain and a few others ran down the road, never looking back. A car suddenly pulled up behind them. "Get in," the driver yelled. He was a recent academy graduate. He drove McCain and the others back to school.

McCain's four years at the academy were rough. He remembers some of the upside: "I hated the place, but I didn't mind going there," he once said. Wearing the dress whites of a midshipman was a plus. Girls flocked to him. When McCain left for a cruise aboard a destroyer in June 1957, the ship docked in Rio de Janeiro in Brazil. He and his classmates caroused for days in the city famous for its nightlife.

Eventually, graduation day came. President Dwight David Eisenhower came to Annapolis to hand out the diplomas. McCain was just one senior in a sea of white as John Poindexter, first in his class, received his scroll. "Congratulations. I hope it won't be too much of a burden for you," the president told Poindexter. McCain graduated 894th out of 899 students. Like father, like son, like grandfather. John McCain was a chip off the old block.

Ironically, 30 years later, Poindexter, the valedictorian of McCain's graduating class, would go on trial for his involvement in a political scandal that overshadowed the presidency of Ronald Reagan. By that time John McCain, nearly last in his class, was a lion of the U.S. Senate.

CHAPTER 4

Flying High

JOHN MCCAIN WAS AN OFFICER, an ensign, in the U.S. Navy. Yet he was not about to let his new rank stop him from having a good time. McCain later wrote, "I enjoyed the off-duty life of a Navy flier more than I enjoyed the actual flying."

McCain's carousing lifestyle was in direct contradiction to the weighty values that the U.S. Naval Academy tried to instill in him. Academy graduates are cloaked in immense responsibility. They are trained to lead others in combat. For an academy graduate, duty and honor are more than words. They are a lifestyle, a calling to be someone better than you are. Members of the U.S. Navy are expected to behave accordingly at all times. If they ever forget, the many monuments placed around the academy remind them of the great responsibility they have undertaken. The inscriptions on those statues can make many midshipmen wonder whether they are good enough to do the job.

It seems that as a young man, John McCain really didn't care.

In August 1958, John Sidney McCain III arrived at the Pensacola Naval Air Station in Florida to begin his training as a pilot. It was a serious undertaking, one that McCain recalls he did not enjoy.

"Graduation transformed neither his style nor his low tolerance for authority," Robert Timberg writes of McCain. "One night he was playing shuffleboard at the Officers' Club. His nondescript outfit included cowboy boots and a chewed-up crewneck sweater.... 'Ensign McCain, your appearance is a disgrace,' said [a senior officer]... 'What do you think your grandfather would say?'"

McCain squinted through the din of the smoky room and mouthed off disrespectfully to the officer. His rebelliousness had not diminished in the least since his days as a cadet.

Into the Wild Blue Yonder

Military pilots are known to be both exacting and risk takers. Their love of flying consumes them and most take to the air whenever possible. They are a competitive bunch and love to "push the envelope," always going faster and higher, sometimes taking chances. McCain, however, was not among that group. He liked flying, but he didn't love it. Being a U.S. Navy fighter pilot did come with a lot of prestige and, for McCain, something more. Being a pilot was, for the young aviator, something his father was not. "Flying was something his father, a submariner, had never done," Timberg writes, "and he wanted to be seen, for better or worse and almost at all costs, as his own man, not Jack McCain's kid."

McCain learned to fly at Pensacola and at the Corpus Christi Naval Air Station in Texas. But his performance was mediocre, not unlike his years at the academy. "McCain was an adequate pilot," Timberg writes, "but he had no patience for studying dry aviation manuals. Instead, he would spend two or three hours each afternoon... reading history.... He worked his way through all three volumes of Gibbon's *Decline and Fall of the Roman Empire*.... He said his father had urged him to do so, told him it was the kind of thing a naval officer should know about."

One Saturday morning McCain was flying over the Gulf of Mexico, practicing landings. Suddenly, his engine quit over Corpus Christi Bay. The plane plunged into the water. The impact knocked McCain out cold. As water rushed into the cockpit of the rapidly sinking plane, he was jolted awake. Still strapped in as the plane settled on the bottom of the bay, McCain was able to free himself, push the plane's canopy loose and swim to the surface. Luckily, he wasn't seriously injured. He was taken to the base hospital, known as sick bay, and examined. X-rays showed no broken bones.

McCain refused to spend the night confined to a sick bay bed so he headed back to his barrack. Later that evening, McCain, rested, headed out for a night of fun with his friends. This was not the first time he'd take a knock and bounce right back. His ability to shake off accident and injury would end up being one of his greatest assets.

McCain made it through flight school alive—barely—and began his tours of duty aboard several aircraft carriers. Ever so slowly, his attitude began to change.

★ ★ ★ ★ ★ ★ ★ ★ ★ ★ ★ ★ ★ ★ ★

Landing on the Deck

There are few things more exciting for a pilot than trying to land a fighter plane on the deck of an aircraft carrier. The small size of a carrier's deck leaves little room for error, whether the plane is being catapulted at tremendous speed on takeoff or landing gingerly on a swaying deck. One careless error or tiny miscalculation could prove catastrophic. An aircraft carrier is always moving—forward, up, down and side to side. And carrier pilots are always practicing, making sure they come in at just the right angle and speed.

Aircraft carriers are equipped with a device that emits a beam of light as the plane approaches. The light is the glide path that pilots have to follow for a safe touchdown. Other devices indicate whether the pilot is above or below the glide path. It is a complicated procedure. The pilot is doing what seems like a hundred things at once—always scanning the landing area of the ship while keeping an eye on the optical glide path.

Cruise Control

"I began to worry a little about my career during my deployments on several Mediterranean cruises in the early sixties," McCain writes.

John McCain, who defied authority at every turn, who dressed like a pauper and ran away from the Shore Patrol, who crashed planes and spent his nights socializing with friends, seemed to be growing up. But what had changed? Simply, he began to enjoy the life of a seaman and Navy flier.

"Like my grandfather and father, I loved life at sea, and I loved flying off carriers," McCain writes. "No other experience in my life so closely approximated the exploits of the brash, daring heroes who had captivated my schoolboy's imagination during those long afternoons in my grandmother's house. Ever since reading about the storied world of men at arms, I had longed for such a life. The Navy…offered the quickest route to adventure if I could manage to avoid committing some career-ending mistake."

John McCain III flew a Douglas A-1 Skyraider while he was a naval aviator.

McCain started acting like he cared, too, not only about his future, but for those around him. He volunteered to stand watch on the bridge, the control house of the massive aircraft carriers. He asked for additional work and eventually trained himself to maneuver the ship at sea. Perhaps being confined to a ship for long periods had something to do with McCain's transformation. Maybe it kept him out of trouble. "I had begun to aspire for more commendable achievements…."

McCain volunteered three times to spend his vacation attending escape and evasion school. The military designed the classes to help downed pilots evade capture. One course was held in the forests of Bavaria, Germany. McCain and several other pilots were given a map and food called "C rations." Their mission was to evade a group of soldiers who were hunting them. The exercise lasted five days and only McCain and one other pilot passed the course. They arrived at their destination, hungry but unharmed.

McCain flew a type of plane called the A-1 Skyraider. The Skyraider was a propeller-driven fighter plane. He and the other pilots in his squadron became close friends. They worked hard and played hard. They spent holidays together. They took shore leave in Europe together.

At times, things got out of hand again. Once McCain was fooling around in the air, flying too low over Spain, and took out some electrical wires. Power went out in hundreds of Spanish homes. The accident made the newspapers. "My daredevil clowning had cut off electricity to a great many Spanish homes and created a small international incident." The papers prominently mentioned that McCain was the son of an admiral. McCain was growing up, but it was a slow process.

Cuban Missile Crisis

When John McCain was at sea in the early 1960s, the United States was mired in the Cold War, in which the Western democracies led by the United States found themselves in an ideologically driven conflict with the communist Soviet Union and its allies. The Cold War created a bipolar world in which the United States and the Soviet Union unofficially vied for power.

In 1959, revolutionary leader Fidel Castro had come to power in the island nation of Cuba, overthrowing the U.S.-backed dictatorship of Fulgencio Batista. Two years later, Castro declared himself a communist. This was a boon to the Soviet Union, which was eager to gain a foothold in the Western Hemisphere. The Soviets immediately embraced Castro, providing Cuba with military advisers, artillery and economic support.

The United States did not like the idea of a Soviet-backed communist state 90 miles from Florida. In April 1961, the Central Intelligence Agency (CIA), the spy agency of the United States, engineered an invasion of the island meant to overthrow the government. Castro's forces slaughtered the invasion force of Cuban exiles recruited by the United States. The situation increased already fraying tensions between the Americans, Soviets and Cubans.

In October 1962, more than a year after the invasion known as the Bay of Pigs, an American spy plane flew a routine reconnaissance mission over Cuba, taking pictures. U.S. intelligence officials determined that the pictures showed that the Cubans, with help from the Russians, were building launch sites for Soviet-made nuclear missiles. The missiles were capable of hitting the United States in minutes. President John F. Kennedy insisted that the Soviet Union remove those missiles. The Soviets stood their ground. The world stood at the brink of nuclear war. The ensuing weeks would come to be known as the Cuban missile crisis.

A Tragedy of the Cold War

The Soviet-made nuclear missiles in Cuba were spotted by what was at the time a secret weapon during the Cold War, an airplane called the U-2. These planes, flying miles high in the atmosphere, were used to spy on the Soviets and their allies.

On the 12th day of the Cuban missile crisis, a U-2 plane, piloted by Air Force Major Rudolf Anderson Jr., was streaking 14 miles above Cuba, taking reconnaissance photos. The Cubans used a Soviet-made surface-to-air missile to shoot down the plane, killing Anderson. It was the pilot's sixth flight during the crisis. His death was the single military casualty of the crisis. For his sacrifice, Anderson was awarded the Air Force Cross.

McCain had just completed a Mediterranean cruise aboard the USS *Enterprise*. The carrier arrived back to its home port in Norfolk, Virginia, and McCain's squadron returned to its home base, the Oceana Naval Air Station. As the fliers settled in, unexpected orders came down the chain of command. McCain and the other pilots were told to fly their planes back to the *Enterprise*. McCain didn't know what was up. His commander simply told him and the others that a hurricane was moving toward the area. The planes had to return to the *Enterprise* for safety reasons.

The explanation sounded strange. The pilots were skeptical. For one thing, no one had heard any news of an approaching storm. Plus, being at sea with a hurricane approaching seemed unwise.

As the *Enterprise* put out to sea, the real reason for the deployment was announced. The pilots assembled in the *Enterprise*'s ready room to listen to a radio broadcast from President Kennedy. The president told the nation about the missiles in Cuba. With the *Enterprise* sailing at full speed ahead, the carrier was going to be part of a "blockade" to stop Soviet ships from reaching Cuba. A confrontation could trigger a nuclear holocaust.

A photograph of the Soviet ship *Metallurg Anosov* alongside the U.S. destroyer *Barry* during the Cuban missile crisis.

"For about five days, the pilots on the *Enterprise* believed we were going into action," McCain remembers. "We had never been in combat before, and despite the global confrontation a strike on Cuba portended, we were prepared and anxious to fly our first mission."

Not only was it a tense time aboard the *Enterprise,* but the world held its breath as the Soviet ships steamed closer. Would they try to run the blockade? Would the Americans respond by firing on, or sinking, a Russian ship? Russian nuclear submarines were in the area. Would they launch their missiles if provoked?

In the end, none of that happened. The Cuban missile crisis, as historians now call it, ended peacefully. The Soviets removed their missiles and the United States guaranteed not to invade Cuba. McCain wasn't disappointed that a showdown never occurred. He knew his time to serve in a combat-related role would come soon or later. "We eagerly anticipated the occasion when we would have the chance to do what we were trained to do, and discover, at least, if we were brave enough for the job."

John McCain would get his chance to prove his bravery soon enough.

CHAPTER 5

A Country at War

THE CUBAN MISSILE CRISIS WAS OVER and John McCain returned to his usual duties. He embarked on his last Mediterranean cruise, marking the end, as he says, of a "completely carefree, unattached, and less than serious Navy flier."

While McCain's father aggressively pursued a career as a flag officer, hoping to mimic his father, John McCain III did not have such ambitions. "Certainly I would have been proud to achieve the feat myself, but I doubt I ever allowed myself to daydream about someday wearing an admiral's stars."

Still, McCain wanted to command. He became more serious about his career. He worried that his youthful antics would block any chance of his commanding a squadron or a carrier, "the pinnacle of a young pilot's aspiration." If he failed to command, McCain lamented, it "would dishonor me and my family."

As it turns out, McCain would have his chance. Tensions in the country of Vietnam were heating up. A war unlike any other was about to start.

Vietnam

If you were to ask average Americans in 1964 where Vietnam was located, chances are they could not find it on a map. Vietnam was a former French colony in Indochina. Beginning in the late 1950s, the United States became increasingly involved in Vietnamese politics, especially after nationalist leader Ho Chi Minh and his communist supporters threw the French out in 1954.

International officials then divided the country to stop a full communist takeover. While the communists ruled the North, a U.S.-backed noncommunist government ruled the South. Ho, however, was determined to unite the country by force. He wanted to make both Vietnams into one communist state.

For its part, the United States believed the South Vietnamese army and its government were too weak to stop the North Vietnamese and the Vietcong, the North's communist allies in the South. As a result, the United States gradually began sending U.S. troops into the region.

These troops were officially called advisers, yet many were U.S. Special Forces units, including the U.S. Navy's SEALs and the U.S. Army's Green Berets. The soldiers began arriving in 1963. At first, their mission was to train the South Vietnamese army. Over time, however, their role increased. The advisers began working with the CIA to ambush enemy supply lines and to capture and kill North Vietnamese officers and Vietcong guerrillas. (Guerrillas are defined as a group of independent fighters using irregular tactics.)

Soon enough Special Forces units began to carry out raids against enemy targets by boat and by helicopter. They also created spy networks in the countryside and cities to acquire information on possible communist infiltrators and their plans.

The United States gradually increased the number of troops as fighting grew more intense. In time, an all-out war engulfed the region. U.S. officials believed that if South Vietnam fell to the communists, other countries in the region would also fall. The Americans called it the domino theory.

Call to Arms

John McCain was in his 20s when American involvement in Vietnam began in earnest. He was part of what historians now call the "Vietnam Generation," those who had come of age in the late 1940s and 1950s. As a child, McCain had silently but intently listened during parties and get-togethers as his father and his friends talked about their exploits during World War II. They spoke of depth-charge attacks and submarine gun battles. McCain noticed that these men did not brag about war to impress each other. On the contrary. They marked their conversations by the lessons of leadership they had learned and how they could apply those lessons to any situation life threw at them.

They also talked about how commanding officers performed in battle. Some were steady leaders. Others did not measure up. McCain's ears perked up when the conversations turned to his father's leadership abilities and the admiration his men had for him.

"They treated him differently, more respectfully than they did one another," McCain remembers. "They often regaled a party with descriptions of my father biting down hard on an unlit cigar in the middle of a fight, unafraid and intensely focused on destroying the enemy.... They talked about how the men under my father's command had been affected by combat, and how my father inspired their confidence in his leadership.... They made military life seem more exciting and attracting to me."

Those stories made a great impression on young John McCain. Like his father and his grandfather, McCain was a warrior, and all warriors desire to go to war. "I wanted to go to Vietnam, and to keep the faith with the family creed," McCain writes. "Anticipating my forthcoming tour in Vietnam, and confident that I could perform credibly in combat, I had begun to believe that I would someday have command of a carrier or squadron. I finally felt that I had settled into the family business and was on my way to a successful career as a naval officer."

But Vietnam and the "family business" would have to take a back seat for a while to a woman named Carol Shepp.

John McCain Marries

Born in 1937, Carol Shepp grew up just outside Philadelphia. John and Carol had known each other since his Annapolis days. Carol, tall and brunette, had dated, and later married, one of McCain's classmates. But in 1964, she was a divorced mother of two small children. McCain and Shepp found each other again when she visited an old friend in Pensacola where McCain was stationed. The two began to date.

"She was attractive, clever and kind, and I was instantly attracted to her," McCain remembers. He was more than happy when she said she also liked him.

By this time, the Navy had assigned McCain as a flight instructor at a naval air base in Meridian, Mississippi. Despite the distance, he flew from Meridian to Philadelphia to spend nearly every weekend with Carol. On July 3, 1965, the two were married. McCain adopted Shepp's children, Doug and Andy, and then the couple had a child of their own, a daughter named Sidney.

John McCain, front right, with members of his squadron in front of his A-4 Skyhawk plane.

McCain made the transition from a rowdy upstart to a settled family man almost seamlessly. He was 28 when he married Carol. Soon after their daughter was born in 1966, McCain was transferred to Jacksonville, Florida, and assigned to a squadron that would leave for Vietnam sometime in 1967.

McCain received his orders in the spring of that year and boarded the aircraft carrier *Forrestal*. He was now flying the A-4 Skyhawk, a delta-wing, single-engine jet fighter. The *Forrestal* sailed across the Mediterranean and through the Suez Canal in Egypt. From there it set a course for the Gulf of Tonkin off the coast of Vietnam. McCain expected to return to his wife and kids within a year. For her part, Carol moved to Europe with the children to await her husband's return. She stopped in London to see John's parents, who were living there at the time, then left for West Germany, Denmark, Holland and Belgium. Her final stop was Garmisch, in southern Germany, where the boys would attend school.

Where He Wanted to Be

The *Forrestal* reached its destination, code-named Yankee Station, about 60 miles off the coast of North Vietnam in the South China Sea. Yankee Station was an important departure point for bombing runs against North Vietnam. At any given time, there were three carriers sitting at Yankee Point conducting air operations for 12 hours a day and 12 hours at night. Pilots of one carrier, for example, would fly from noon to midnight, while pilots from another would operate from midnight to noon.

When McCain arrived on the *Forrestal,* the United States was two years into a relentless bombing campaign against North Vietnam. From 1965 to 1968, Operation Rolling Thunder, as it was called, resulted in the destruction of many targets, including bridges, ammunition depots and airfields in the North. President Lyndon Johnson, along with his military advisers, selected the targets to be bombed, sometimes over lunch at the White House. The goal of the bombing campaign was not necessarily to win a military victory, but to break the spirit and morale of the North Vietnamese people who were supporting their military. As a result, hundreds of thousands of North Vietnamese civilians were killed along with military personnel.

McCain wanted to fly as many combat missions as the Navy would assign because he knew that no naval aviator could ascend the Navy's career ladder without them. In many respects, it was good duty. Carrier-based pilots flew missions that lasted no more than an hour from takeoff to landing. The minutes in between were harrowing, dangerous and exhilarating.

McCain's A-4 Skyhawk was a workhorse. Designed in the 1950s, the A-4 could carry up to 9,900 pounds of firepower. To make sure the planes could fly great distances, mechanics fitted the aircraft with an exterior 200-gallon fuel tank. When the Skyhawk squadrons took off, they were chased by F-4 Phantoms that flew cover for them, ready to shoot down incoming surface-to-air missiles, hit missile sites on the ground or engage an occasional Soviet-made MiG, the plane that North Vietnamese pilots flew.

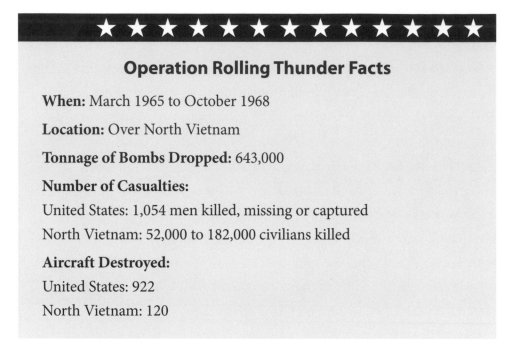

★ ★ ★ ★ ★ ★ ★ ★ ★ ★ ★ ★ ★ ★ ★ ★

Operation Rolling Thunder Facts

When: March 1965 to October 1968

Location: Over North Vietnam

Tonnage of Bombs Dropped: 643,000

Number of Casualties:
United States: 1,054 men killed, missing or captured
North Vietnam: 52,000 to 182,000 civilians killed

Aircraft Destroyed:
United States: 922
North Vietnam: 120

Fire!

On the morning of July 19, 1967, McCain readied for his next scheduled sortie, as the bombing missions were called. It was about 11 a.m., and McCain was waiting for his turn to take off from the *Forrestal*'s flight deck. Tom Ott, a second-class petty officer, was McCain's parachute rigger. His job was to maintain and prepare the equipment on the aircraft for the pilots. McCain had often complained that he found it difficult to see through the visor of his helmet. Before McCain took off on every mission, one thing Ott would do is clean McCain's visor one last time.

"I was a thirty-one-year-old A-4 pilot, and like most pilots I was a little superstitious," McCain remembers. "I had flown five bombing runs over North Vietnam without incident, and I preferred that all preflight tasks be performed in the same order as my previous missions, believing any unvarying routine portended a safe flight. Wiping my visor was one of the tasks executed in that routine."

On the other side of the deck that day, workers hooked up a F-4 Phantom to a generator to jump-start its engine. The F-4 carried a Zuni rocket that Phantom pilots fired in air-to-air combat and air-to-ground operations.

As the F-4 charged up, McCain's A-4 roared to life, and McCain continued to go over his preflight checklist. On this particular day, Ott did as he had always done. He cleaned the visor and then gave the helmet back to McCain. Ott flashed the thumbs-up sign that meant everything was okay. He then shut the canopy of McCain's A-4 and started to walk away from the plane. All systems were go.

Just then, the pilot of the F-4 pressed a button on his control panel. The button switched the aircraft from external to internal power. The action was so routine that the pilot didn't think twice about it. On this day, though, disaster struck. Unknown to the pilot, someone had attached a small electrical wire to a Phantom's Zuni rocket. The small wire, known as a pigtail, carried the electrical charge that fired the rockets. But for safety reasons, the pigtail was not supposed to be hooked up to the rocket until just before the plane was about to take off.

Once the pilot pushed the power button, an electrical charge flashed through the pigtail. The Zuni ignited beneath the Phantom's wing and launched. McCain didn't see the missile coming. The rocket punched a hole through the exterior fuel tank of McCain's A-4.

The jolt was as tremendous as it was unexpected. The explosion was deafening. Two hundred gallons of extremely combustible aviation fuel poured out onto the flight deck, igniting as it flowed along. Black smoke began billowing from the *Forrestal*.

"I opened my canopy, raced to the nose, crawled out onto the refueling probe, and jumped ten feet into the fire," McCain writes. "I rolled through a wall of flames as my flight suit caught fire. I put the flames out and ran as fast as I could to the starboard side of the deck."

Smoke billows from the F-4 Phantom explosion
that ignited the fire aboard the USS *Forrestal*.

The A-4 pilot next to McCain's plane also jumped from his open canopy into the fire, his suit engulfed in flames. McCain rushed to help as several crewmen grabbed a fire hose and started dragging it toward the fire. One sailor ran with a portable fire extinguisher to spray the 1,000-pound bombs that the rocket's impact had dislodged from McCain's plane.

Seconds later, the heat from the fire ignited the bombs. They exploded in heart-thumping, ear-splitting crescendo. The sailor with the fire extinguisher was killed. The explosion blew McCain backward. Small pieces of shrapnel tore through his legs and chest.

The fire swept the deck of the ship as more bombs exploded. McCain was injured, bloody, but alive. Many others weren't so lucky. They perished in the explosion and the resulting blaze. The carnage was horrifying. The pilot McCain was trying to help died in the blast. The men dragging the hose to put out the flames were incinerated. Other planes on the deck exploded. The immense heat triggered ejection seats that flew through the air, hitting the water and the ship's deck with a tremendous thud. Some pilots were still sitting in them.

More bombs exploded. The heat caused more Zuni rockets to fire, shooting across the ship. Explosions blasted holes into the deck of the *Forrestal*. Crewmen quickly manned forklifts and tried to push burning planes into the South China Sea. Fuel spilled from the deck down to the hangar below, igniting even more fires. Crew members tried frantically to unload a cache of bombs from the flight elevator before the flames reached them. The true-to-life nightmare seemed as if it would never end.

"The fires were consuming the *Forrestal*. I thought she might sink. But the crew's heroics kept her afloat," McCain writes. "Men sacrificed their lives for one another and for the ship. Many of them were only eighteen and nineteen years old. They fought the inferno with the tenacity usually reserved for hand-to-hand combat. They fought it all day and well into the next, and they saved the *Forrestal*."

The wounded McCain limped to sick bay. Inside, the scene was grisly. Men were dying, their bodies charred beyond recognition. Some prayed silently as they waited for death. A young seaman called out to McCain. McCain did not recognize the boy because of his injuries. The seaman asked if a certain pilot in McCain's squadron had survived. McCain said he had. The young sailor died, his last words forever etched on McCain's mind: "Thank God."

Three days later, the *New York Times* announced the disaster in a front-page headline: "At Least 70 Dead in Forrestal Fire; 89 Others Missing." Reporter R.W. Apple wrote the story: "Not until 8:30 last night, nearly 10 hours after it broke out, was the fire brought under control, the Navy reported. The last flames were not extinguished until 12:20 a.m. today.... The 75,900-ton carrier, nearly 12 years old, was said to have suffered extensive damage. Four holes were blown in her flight deck by exploding 750-pound bombs.... Four more holes had to be cut in the deck to fight the stubborn flames, which swept through the maze of cables and piping between the flight deck and the hangar deck below."

In total, the fire killed 134 men including Tom Ott, McCain's parachute rigger who seconds before had given the thumbs-up signal. The *Forrestal* fire was a disaster that would live in the memories of those who survived for the rest of their lives.

"We were given masks and gloves and took the bodies out in bags and gave them to the corpsmen," retired Rear Admiral Peter Booth told *USA Today,* in a 2017 article that marked the 50th anniversary of the fire. It was dark out, Booth said, and he remembered that he and others mistakenly put two corpses in one bag. "It was a difficult thing to do."

Movies and photos taken that day show the carnage. It was the worst fire on an aircraft carrier since World War II. With 20 planes destroyed and several large holes in its hull below the waterline, the *Forrestal* limped to the Philippines for repairs. It was a slow trip. When the carrier reached Subic Bay, workers repaired the ship just enough so it could sail back to the United States. It took two years to completely repair the damage, but the *Forrestal* eventually made its way back to the sea.

The fire was a pivotal moment in McCain's life. He thought his time at war was over. He was saddened, thinking that he would not fulfill his promise of serving his country. "I did not take a perverse pleasure in the terror and destruction of war," he writes. "I did not delight in the brief, intense thrill of flying combat missions. I was gratified when my bombs hit their target, but I did not particularly enjoy the excitement of the experience...the purpose of my years of training had been to prepare me for this moment. As the crippled *Forrestal* limped toward port, my moment was disappearing when it had barely begun, and I feared my ambitions were among the casualties in the calamity that had claimed the *Forrestal*."

CHAPTER 6

A New Ship

WITH THE *FORRESTAL* OUT OF COMMISSION, John McCain had nowhere to go. Shortly after the fire, an officer from the USS *Oriskany* talked to McCain and the rest of his squadron. He asked if they wanted to volunteer for duty aboard the carrier. McCain and a few of the others signed up. Then they waited for the Navy's approval.

With nothing to do but wait, McCain toured Hawaii, where the crew had gone after the fire, then traveled to London to see his father and mother. Carol and the kids were still touring Europe at that time. McCain eventually met them in Cannes, France, where a hotel offered free lodging for those who had served aboard the *Forrestal*. The ship had been a common sight in France's ports of call over the years, and the French hotel wanted to show its appreciation.

McCain cherished this European vacation. The family went on sightseeing trips. At night, John and Carol sometimes visited places where McCain had been before. In several of these restaurants and saloons, guests, employees and owners recognized the flier. They crowded around McCain, happy to see him.

Despite the respite, McCain grew increasingly concerned because his orders had yet to arrive. He worried that the Navy did not want anything to do with him. McCain knew that wherever he went, whatever unit he was part of, his bad-boy reputation preceded him. "I may have to get out of the Navy," he told a friend.

Finally, McCain's orders arrived. The Navy had indeed assigned him to the *Oriskany,* an attack carrier named for a Revolutionary War battle fought in upstate New York in 1777. "I was relieved at this unexpected change in my fortunes," McCain writes.

Anticipating his assignment, McCain moved with his family near Jacksonville, Florida, where they rented a house in nearby Orange Park. McCain waited for his final orders to arrive. When they did, the plan was for Carol and his family to stay in Orange Park until McCain came home for good.

McCain was happy to be serving aboard a new vessel. The *Oriskany* was one of the Navy's chief weapons during the Cold War. Built by the New York Naval Ship Yard in the late 1940s, the ship had been commissioned in 1950, giving the Navy's Sixth Fleet a strong presence in the Mediterranean and the Near East.

When the Korean War began in 1950, the *Oriskany*'s pilots flew bombing and strafing attacks (when low-flying planes attack with machine-gun fire) against enemy supply lines. By April 1965, the *Oriskany* was once again in the thick of battle, this time in Vietnam. But it was a snake-bitten ship, meaning it had bad luck. On October 26, 1966, a fire broke out aboard the *Oriskany,* ignited by multiple flares stored in a locker. The blaze killed 44 people and injured 156.

"The *Oriskany* was regarded as a dangerous place to live," McCain said.

The U.S. Navy aircraft carrier, the USS *Oriskany*.

The War Escalates

By the time McCain reported for duty on September 30, 1967, the Vietnam War was entering a new, deadlier phase. The first U.S. combat troops had waded ashore on the beaches of Danang, South Vietnam, in 1965. By the end of that year, there were 189,000 American troops stationed in Vietnam. By 1966, that number had nearly doubled. As a result, casualties increased.

Vietnam was like no other war in American history. There were no front lines as there had been in World War I, World War II and the Korean War. Instead, enemy fighters, the Vietcong, were all around. They often wore black, pajama-like outfits. They hid in the hills, dug tunnels into the mountains as a place to hide, escape, and store their equipment. They blended in with the rest of the civilian population.

To root them out, the Americans went on so-called search-and-destroy missions in the jungle. Soldiers also moved into village after village, looking for any signs of Vietcong activity. Many of the battles fought by the Americans were skirmishes or ambushes, usually involving only a handful of troops. There were, however, a few large-scale battles with groups of Vietcong and North Vietnamese army regulars. By 1967, nearly 100 U.S. soldiers were dying each week. By the end of that year, nearly 500,000 U.S. combat troops were stationed in Vietnam.

Moreover, Operation Rolling Thunder, the air bombing campaign begun in 1965, was going strong. As the bombing increased, the North Vietnamese beefed up their defenses around Hanoi, the country's capital, and other key cities.

★ ★ ★ ★ ★ ★ ★ ★ ★ ★ ★ ★ ★ ★ ★ ★

Surface-to-Air Missiles

One of the most potent air defense systems the North Vietnamese had in their arsenal were Soviet-made surface-to-air missiles, known as SAMs. In 1964, as the United States became increasingly involved in Vietnam, the Soviets decided to support the communist government, giving the North SAMs and MiG fighter jets. The SAMs could quickly accelerate to 3.5 times the speed of sound, or Mach 3.5, hitting targets flying as high as 50,000 feet. Each had a range of 25 miles. If an American plane was flying under 3,000 feet, the SAMs were largely useless. Soviet advisers, wearing North Vietnamese uniforms, trained the missile crews.

Construction of the first SAM site did not begin until April 1965. The SAMs arrived from the Soviet Union through Haiphong Harbor. When McCain flew over the harbor, he watched as workers unloaded the missiles off the Soviet ships. "We could see the SAMs being transported to firing sites and put into place," he said.

But there was nothing McCain or the other pilots could do about it. President Johnson was fearful of destroying a Soviet ship, lest the Soviets retaliate, a situation that could involve the use of nuclear weapons. Instead, American pilots could shoot at the SAM sites only if the missiles were firing on them.

The Saints

When McCain boarded the *Oriskany,* he joined an A-4 group called the Saints. In 1967, one-third of the squadron's pilots had been either killed or captured. Saints pilots might have had a high casualty rate but it wasn't because they weren't skilled. They were an aggressive squad of fliers. Just prior to McCain joining the group, the Saints had destroyed all the bridges in Haiphong, an important port.

The Saints were equipped with Walleye smart bombs, a television-guided explosive that could hit targets with precision. Engineers had designed the Walleyes to reduce so-called collateral damage—the killing of civilians and the destruction of hospitals and schools.

Pilots took it hard when their fellow crew members failed to make it back to the *Oriskany* safely. Yet McCain and the others understood the risks of the job. McCain writes there was an "indifference to death that masked a great sadness in the squadron, a sadness that grew more pervasive as our casualty list lengthened. But we kept our game faces on, and our bravado became all the more exaggerated when the squadron returned to ship after a mission with one or more missing planes. We flew the next raid with greater determination to do as much damage as we could, repeating to ourselves before the launch, 'If we destroy the target, we don't have to go back.'"

Though McCain always had his "game face" on, he knew death or capture was a real possibility. During one raid over Haiphong, McCain was the third pilot flying with the squadron commander, Bryan Compton. As they flew over the target, the North Vietnamese shot down the number two pilot. McCain and Compton watched in the hopes that they would see the pilot eject from his injured plane and parachute safely to the ground.

Compton circled the harbor low in the sky, at only 2,000 feet or so, looking for any sign of the downed pilot. In the meantime, McCain and Compton were taking heavy fire, or "flak," from ground-based guns. The North Vietnamese were also firing SAMs. "I was scared to death waiting for Bryan to call off the search and lead us back to the *Oriskany* and out of harm's way."

Compton made six, seven, eight sweeps before he gave up the search. His courage inspired McCain. "I remembered what I saw that day. I saw a courageous squadron commander put his life in grave peril so that a friend's family might know if their loved one was alive or dead. For his heroics and his ability to survive, the rest of the squadron regarded Bryan as indestructible. We were proud to serve under his command."

October 26, 1967

On October 26, 1967, John McCain was preparing to make his twenty-third bombing run over North Vietnam. He had been on the *Oriskany* for only a month. The previous day, McCain had destroyed three MiG fighters sitting on the tarmac of the Phuc Yen Airfield, the largest air base in the North, located 18 miles northwest of the capital city. The base was home to at least 1,000 MiGs, many anti-aircraft guns and more than a dozen SAM sites. In addition, there were thousands of people on the ground, all armed with rifles, all waiting to take their shot at the incoming Americans.

Air Force F-105 Thunderchief pilots drop bombs over North Vietnam in 1966.

The attack on Phuc Yen was important not just because it was a successful raid, but because it was part of a major escalation of Operation Rolling Thunder. Until that point, U.S. pilots were mainly confined to bombing trucks, trains, barges and bridges. That strategy had proved useless. Instead of destroying the enemy's morale, it made the North Vietnamese angrier and more resilient.

"When I was on the *Forrestal,* every man in my squadron had thought Washington's air war plans were senseless," McCain admits. "The night before my first mission, I had gone up to the squadron's intelligence center to punch out information on my target. Out came a picture of a military barracks, with some details about the target's recent history. It had already been bombed twenty-seven times."

When the men of the *Oriskany* received their orders to step up the bombing campaign, they were more than happy to oblige. "For the first time we believed we were helping to win the war, and we were proud to be usefully employed."

McCain's mission on October 26 was aimed not at the airfield, but at a power plant in Hanoi. It was a major raid and involved McCain's A-4 squadron and another group of A-4s nicknamed the Ghost Riders. A number of F-8s would escort the A-4s.

McCain wasn't supposed to fly this particular mission, but he had pleaded with the squadron's operation officer to include him in the strike. An earlier raid had destroyed the power plant, but now it was back up and running. Its destruction was a source of pride for the Saints. McCain, by his own admission, was feeling cocky that day. He was proud of his work over Phuc Yen the day before. "I was still charged up from the previous day's good fortune, and was anticipating more success that morning despite having been warned about Hanoi's extensive air defense system," McCain writes.

Hanoi had the most formidable air defense system in the history of modern warfare up until that point. As McCain and the other pilots walked out of the *Oriskany*'s ready room, Lew Chatman, the carrier's strike officer, said, "You'd better be careful. We're probably going to lose someone on this one."

McCain looked back at Chatman and said, "You don't have to worry about me, Lew."

CHAPTER 7

Shot Down Over Hanoi

A FEW DAYS AFTER John Sidney McCain III lived through the *Forrestal* fire, he sat down with a reporter from the *New York Times* and some of his friends to discuss the tragedy. The group gathered at the reporter's villa in Saigon, the capital of South Vietnam. "It's a difficult thing to say," McCain said. "But now that I've seen what the bombs…did to the people on our ship, I'm not so sure that I want to drop any more of that stuff on North Vietnam."

Still, McCain understood his duty, and he headed back to war on the *Oriskany*. "As he suggested that night in July," the *Times* reporter wrote, "it may have been because he had no other trade. His grandfather had been a full admiral—four stars—and his father was one, too. No other family in the long history of the American Navy could boast such a singular tradition."

When the reporter asked if McCain thought that being captured by the North Vietnamese would be worse than the *Forrestal* fire, McCain thought for a second. "No," he said, "I don't think so. Pilots get paid to take chances. We're all professional military men and I suppose that it's our war."

Which is exactly why on October 26, 1967, John McCain climbed aboard his A-4, received the thumbs-up sign and catapulted off the

Oriskany's deck. Miles away a power plant in Hanoi was waiting to be destroyed. Once the squadron flew off the carrier's deck, they headed west of the capital city. The mission called for the pilots to then make a turn, at which point they would begin their bombing run. "We came in from the west so that once we had rolled in on the target, released our bombs, and pulled out we would be flying directly over the Tonkin Gulf" and back home to the *Oriskany*, McCain remembered in his memoir.

The A-4s were amazing machines. They were small. They were agile. They were light. Yet they could carry nearly 10,000 pounds of bombs, rockets and missiles. Mounted on each wing was a 20-millimeter cannon that had a tendency to jam. The planes also came equipped with "countermeasures," electronic devices that could fool incoming surface-to-air missiles. Instead of chasing the heat signature created by the plane's engines, the SAMs followed the countermeasures instead.

Engineers also equipped the planes with sophisticated radar detection systems. If the plane's radar spotted an incoming SAM, its lights would flash and alarms would sound. One tone meant a missile's radar had homed in on the plane; others sounded when the missile had locked onto the aircraft and was about to hit.

Flight Over Hanoi

McCain's squadron flew in formation toward Hanoi on its dangerous mission. At about 9,000 feet, McCain turned toward the target. That's when the warning lights flashed, telling the flier that a SAM radar had his plane in its sights. A missile firing was only moments away. The alarm was so loud that McCain had to turn down the volume.

As he got closer to the city, McCain saw huge clouds of black smoke and dust billowing from the ground. The North Vietnamese had launched their missiles. The closer the bombers got, the more anti-aircraft flak they encountered from ground-based guns. "For the first time in combat I saw thick black clouds of anti-aircraft flak everywhere, images familiar to me only from World War II movies."

North Vietnamese soldier preparing to fire an SA-7 surface-to-air missile.

But this wasn't Hollywood make-believe. The SAMs were real, as large as a "flying telephone pole," McCain said. "They scared the hell out of me."

These "flying telephone poles" were moving quickly. The North Vietnamese would fire 22 of them that day. The closer the A-4s got to Hanoi, the darker the sky became with smoke from anti-aircraft bursts. Each pilot called out on the radio anytime he saw a missile coming his way.

McCain flew as he had never flown before, using all his skills and ability to avoid a hit. Finally, amid the smoke he recognized the target, the power plant, near a small lake. He put his plane into a dive and steeled himself to deliver its destructive ordnance.

Time to "Jink"?

Suddenly, the sound no pilot wants to hear filled McCain's cockpit. A SAM had locked onto his A-4. Normally, McCain would have flown evasively, "jinking," as pilots called it, in order to escape. He should have rolled out of the dive. It wasn't a big deal for the A-4 to outrun and outmaneuver a SAM. Plus, the plane could take a pounding. Many A-4s had returned to their carriers shot up but otherwise in one piece. The A-4 would take more punishment from the force of gravity than a SAM could. All McCain had to do was pull up on the stick and fly safely away.

"I was just about to release my bombs when the tone sounded, and had I started jinking I would never have the time, nor probably, the nerve, to go back in once I had lost the SAM," he said.

At around 3,500 feet, McCain released his bombs. He quickly pulled back on the stick and climbed fast and steep. He was hoping to put some distance between him and the incoming SAM. Before the plane could react, the SAM hit, blowing off one of the A-4's wings. One of the F-8 escorts was also shot down.

"I knew I was hit," McCain recalled. "My A-4, traveling about 550 miles an hour, was violently spiraling to earth."

The A-4 was out of control, falling toward earth. McCain was well-trained. Though adrenaline flushed his body and his heart pounded, he wasn't fearful, and he kept his cool. "I didn't think, 'Gee, I'm hit—what now?'" He looked out and saw the damage. He knew he was in trouble. He barked on the radio, "I'm hit."

McCain would later explain to a reporter that "things were happening too fast. I heard a terrible explosion which shook my plane and sent it toward the ground. It was hit so violently that I was thrown on my back and went straight toward the ground.... I tried to pull the direction stick to reestablish the balance of my plane, but it no longer responded."

There was only one thing McCain could do. He reached up and pulled the ejection seat handle. As McCain pulled the lever, the A-4's canopy blew off. Then small rockets exploded, sending McCain flying out of the dying aircraft. As he bounded into the air, McCain's hands flailed wildly. "I do not know at what altitude, but it must have been very low," McCain told the reporter. "Naturally I felt buffeting because my bailing out was made at the time when the plane was falling too fast."

McCain's body struck the plane, breaking his left arm, his right arm, and his right knee, which probably hit the plane's control panel when he was thrown from the cockpit. McCain was in imminent danger and it was not going to get any better anytime soon. The force of the ejection knocked him out for a minute. His parachute barely opened before McCain struck the shallow water of Truc Bach Lake. Escape was impossible. The injured

Navy pilot was in the middle of the enemy's capital city in the bright light of day.

McCain regained consciousness just before hitting the water. "When the parachute opened, I looked down and found that I was going to fall into a lake," McCain told the reporter. "I was really lucky to be able to fall into a lake. All around me bombs were exploding while rockets and anti-aircraft shells were streaking through the sky."

John McCain (center on his back) is pulled from the water after crashing into Truc Bach Lake in Vietnam.

Then he sank to the lake bottom, weighted down by 50 pounds of gear. Still, McCain managed to extricate himself and swim to the top. He didn't feel any pain once he broke the surface, but he couldn't understand why he couldn't inflate his life vest. His arms wouldn't move. He sank to the bottom of the lake again and once again surfaced. Finally, using his teeth, McCain pulled the toggle that inflated the life vest. Then all went black again.

★ ★ ★ ★ ★ ★ ★ ★ ★ ★ ★ ★ ★ ★ ★ ★

Dateline Hanoi

The press, for the most part, had unfettered access to the battlefield in Vietnam. This is how a French reporter, Bernard-Joseph Cabanes, of the French Press Agency, described the October 26 raid on Hanoi:

U.S. aircraft today attacked Hanoi for the second day running, concentrating on the electric power plant. But several rockets landed in other parts of the city as well, destroying houses and inflicting what was believed to be higher casualties than yesterday's raid. Missiles brought down two of the attacking planes over the center of the city. An open parachute was seen floating amid the puff of exploding anti-aircraft shells. An air-to-ground missile struck a house in the Hue Street district, subjected to bombing last August. The house was 50 yards from the French diplomatic delegation where shrapnel fell in the garden today. No French were injured.

CHAPTER 8

Prisoner

MCCAIN WOKE UP AND WHAT HE SAW SCARED HIM. Twenty angry
North Vietnamese were pulling him from the water. By this time, hundreds
had gathered along the banks of the lake. Dazed, injured and bleeding,
McCain heard angry shouts from the mob as he was carried ashore on
a bamboo stretcher that his captors had rigged together. As they set the
stretcher down, the mob ripped his flight suit from his body. McCain,
wearing nothing but his skivvies, was kicked and punched, spat on and
shouted at. In pain, he looked down and saw that his right foot was resting
next to his left knee in an unnatural position. "My God, my leg," he
screamed.

Just then someone smashed him in the shoulder with the butt of a rifle.
Someone else stuck a bayonet into his ankle and groin. Suddenly, a woman
started yelling at the angry horde. She demanded they stop attacking the
pilot. The crowd backed off. She then took pieces of bamboo and made
splints for McCain's leg and right arm.

Finally, North Vietnamese soldiers came, and McCain breathed a sigh
of relief. "I noticed an army truck arrive on the scene to take me away

from this group of aggrieved citizens who seemed intent on killing me," he writes in his memoir. "Before they put me in the back of the truck, the woman who had stopped the crowd from killing me held a cup of tea to my lips while photographers recorded the act. The solders then placed me on a stretcher, loaded me into the truck, and drove me a few blocks to an ocher-colored, trapezoid-shape stone structure that occupied two city blocks in the center of downtown Hanoi."

The soldiers carried McCain through the enormous steel gates of the old French prison that American prisoners of war called the "Hanoi Hilton." (The Hilton Hotel chain is popular in the United States.) As McCain heard the gates clank shut, a sense of despair coursed through his battered body. "I felt a deeper dread than I have ever felt since."

McCain's captors took him to an empty cell and put the stretcher on the floor. He was still in his underwear. Someone covered him with a blanket. That lonely room was where McCain stayed for several days, drifting into and out of consciousness. His wounds were crudely bandaged but his broken bones were not set. McCain was now a prisoner of war, or POW.

★ ★ ★ ★ ★ ★ ★ ★ ★ ★ ★ ★ ★ ★ ★ ★

Heavy Losses

In addition to John McCain, many Navy and Marine fliers flew the A-4 Skyhawk during the Vietnam War. The losses for each were staggering. The Navy lost 37 percent of its A-4s, while the Marines lost 36 percent.

Interrogation

In his lucid moments when McCain was conscious, his captors took him into an empty room and started asking questions. They demanded military information, such as what type of aircraft he had flown. What were his intended future targets? Answer the questions, his interrogators cajoled, and he'd be given medical treatment.

At first, McCain refused to give any information beyond his name, rank, date of birth, and military serial number. "The information was of no real use to the Vietnamese, but the Code of Conduct for American Prisoners of War orders us to refrain from providing any information beyond our name, rank, and serial number," McCain writes.

The North Vietnamese beat him again and again, hoping to elicit a response more to their liking. Sharp pain ripped through McCain's broken limbs with each beating. He blacked out, only to come to again and receive the same punishment. In his mind, McCain promised he wasn't going to let the enemy get the best of him. "I thought if I could hold out like this for a few days, they would relent and take me to a hospital."

The questions continued. The answers did not. The beatings were a nearly everyday affair. A guard fed him twice a day, but McCain was unable to hold down food. He vomited on the floor. He was thirsty all the time. His lips were dry and cracked. Only occasional sips of tea helped hydrate his body. When the guards pulled the blanket from his legs, McCain saw how bad his knee was. It was swollen and discolored, the blood pooling underneath his skin. He developed a fever and remained unconscious for hours at a time.

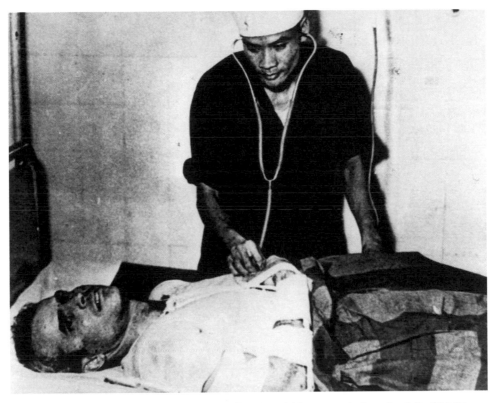

John McCain is examined at a hospital in Hanoi, Vietnam, during the fall of 1967.

Finally, a North Vietnamese army officer known as Bug to the other POWs arrived to question McCain. Bug spoke some English. He was short and heavy. And mean. McCain tried to bargain with him, but Bug ignored the soldier's words. "Take me to the hospital and I'll give you all the information you want," McCain lied. He believed if he could just get a bit stronger, he could endure any punishment the North Vietnamese handed out. Finally, the camp doctor came into the room.

"Are you going to take me to the hospital?" McCain asked.

"No," Bug replied. "It's too late."

McCain panicked and believed he was going to die. But he eventually got the care he needed when the North Vietnamese figured out who he was. "Your father is a big admiral?" Bug asked in broken English.

Yes, McCain answered.

"Now we take you to the hospital."

McCain passed out as his captors moved him. When he awoke in a hospital bed, he saw that his surroundings were filthy. Disease-carrying mosquitoes swarmed and rats ran across a floor covered in puddles of water from the rain that poured down incessantly. McCain was given intravenous life-sustaining glucose, a form of sugar, and blood transfusions.

News Arrives

John and Roberta McCain were in London dressing for a dinner party at the Iranian ambassador's residence when the phone rang. On the other end was an official at the Pentagon. He told the admiral two planes had been shot down during a raid over Hanoi. Their son John was the pilot on one of the aircraft.

John Jr., a four-star admiral, broke the news to his wife. The two talked about what they should do next. They decided it was best to keep up appearances and attend the dinner party. "We're going to go and we're going to keep our mouths shut," Admiral McCain said. John's parents then called his wife Carol, who had already been notified.

John's mother, ever the military wife and pragmatic mother, knew how such things played out. She tried to prepare Carol. Johnny, as she called him, was probably dead, and everyone in the family would have to accept that fact, she told her daughter-in-law.

"I don't intend to," Carol said.

Calls then went out to John's sister and brother.

"Honey, Johnny's been shot down," Roberta told her son, Joe, John's younger brother, who was then working as a reporter for the *San Diego Tribune*.

"What happened?" Joe asked.

Roberta told him. "His wingman saw his plane explode. They don't think he got out."

An aerial view of the Hanoi Hilton, the infamous North Vietnamese POW camp.

Joe started to cry. "What do we do now?" he asked.

"Pray for him, my boy," his father said.

And pray they did. The next day, R.W. Apple, John McCain's friend at the *New York Times,* filed a dispatch from Saigon, in South Vietnam. The headline read: "Adm. McCain's son, Forrestal Survivor, is Missing in Raid."

Although the headline was somewhat misleading—McCain wasn't missing—it provided some details and gave his parents and wife a lifeline of hope. Apple explained that McCain had indeed survived the crash, although his condition was not known:

> *[A] North Vietnamese broadcast said that Commander McCain had been "blasted down by a ground-to-air missile before the plane could strike." The plane, Hanoi said, crashed into the compound of a factory—perhaps the cement plant near the power station—and McCain fell into nearby Trucbach Lake.*
>
> *From an observation post on the shore of the lake . . . a shot rang out: "Get him! Get him right away!" The broadcast said that Commander McCain had been shot in the leg while still in his airplane. Before being taken to a detention camp, he was said to have been treated by a nurse for his wounds. "Many people who happened to be on the scene swam toward the fallen air pirate," the broadcast went on. Four of his captors hauled him up. Two locked both his arms while others put his head on a bamboo tube to keep him afloat.*

Just under that story an Associated Press report quoted the Pentagon that McCain had been indeed captured.

Of course, no one had to tell John McCain that.

Slowly Recovering

Slowly the Navy aviator recovered. He lay in the hospital bed filthy, unshaved and unwashed. Although tubes ran into his arms, no one had yet treated his broken bones. But, as he became stronger and more coherent, his interrogators resumed their work. They continued to demand information. If McCain did not oblige, they would stop whatever meager medical treatment he was receiving.

McCain started to open up to his captors. He gave them his ship's name and the squadron number. He also confirmed that the power plant had been that day's target. But the interrogators wanted the names of those in McCain's squadron. McCain wasn't about to divulge the identities of his fellow airmen. Instead, he gave his captors the names of offensive linemen on the Green Bay Packers football team. When the questions continued with "What other targets were you going to strike?" he lied and mentioned only the North Vietnamese cities he had already attacked.

When McClain declined to give them any more information, the North Vietnamese beat him senseless. Each blow led to excruciating pain. Finally, the beatings ceased. "My interrogators appeared concerned that hospital personnel might object."

Used for Propaganda

McCain came to realize that the treatment he received, although brutal and harsh, was less than what other American POWs had gone through. "Later, my suspicion was confirmed when I heard accounts of other POWs' experiences during their first interrogation. They had endured far worse than I had, and had withstood the cruelest torture imaginable."

McCain's father, after all, was an admiral, and that high rank provided a shield of sorts that minimized the beatings. McCain, because of his bloodline, was valuable to the communists. They could use him as a tool in their propaganda campaign. The North Vietnamese didn't want McCain too badly hurt and certainty didn't want him dead. He was more valuable to them alive than in a grave.

McCain rarely saw a doctor or nurse, but was constantly shadowed by a teenage boy. McCain could not feed himself, so the teen spoon-fed him a bowl of tasteless noodles. After about a week of his confinement in the hospital, a doctor finally attempted to set McCain's broken right arm. The doctor did not administer any anesthesia. He didn't have to. The pain of the treatment was so bad that it rendered McCain unconscious. The procedure proved to be too difficult and unwieldy for the doctor. He decided to mold a heavy plaster cast around McCain's arm and torso. With no cotton lining, the cast rubbed painfully against McCain's skin. It eventually wore two holes down to the bone.

One day a French television reporter, François Chalais, visited McCain. Chalais wanted to film an interview with McCain. He said he would carry a message back to McCain's family. In reality, Chalais was a puppet used by the North Vietnamese, whom he sympathized with. He hoped that an interview with McCain would help morale in the North and perhaps turn Americans in the United States against the war.

At first, McCain balked at the idea. But he was anxious to let his family know that he was alive. His captors said that, if he agreed to the interview, they would operate again on his broken body. "You will say you're grateful to the Vietnamese people and that you're sorry for your crimes," they told him.

McCain said no once again, but finally gave in when he figured that his captors would send him back to the prison camp if he didn't agree. The interview was filmed by two cameramen and lasted four minutes. On the black-and-white film, McCain looked as if he were drugged and in pain. In response to Chalais' questions, McCain said he was treated well by his captors. When Chalais asked him about the food he received, McCain replied with a flash of his ever-present smart-aleck humor, "It's not like Paris... [but] I eat it." He then told Chalais the details of being shot down.

"Was there anything else you would like to say?" the reporter asked. McCain's voice choked with emotion. Tears welled in the young man's eyes. "I would like to tell my wife that I'm going to get well, I love her and I hope to see her soon. I would appreciate it if you tell her that. That's all."

The North Vietnamese army officer supervising the interview was a man McCain called Chihuahua. He did not like McCain's answers. He had not followed orders about what he should and should not say. "Chihuahua told me to say that I could receive letters and pictures from home." McCain said no, refusing to lie.

In the room was another officer, Major Nguyen Bai, the commandant of the North Vietnamese prison system. His nickname was Cat. Cat was also extremely upset with McCain's answers. He "demanded that I say on camera how much I wanted the war to end so I could go home.... Although I had resisted giving my interrogators any useful information and had greatly irritated the Cat by refusing his demands during the interview, I should not have given out information about my ship and squadron, and I regret very much having done so."

Cat was incensed and berated McCain for his "bad attitude": "He told me I would not receive any more operations." Guards then spirited McCain off to his old room in the hospital.

The broadcast was seen in France and on CBS in the United States. McCain's family saw the interview before it was aired. It was a relief for them to know John was alive and recuperating, as far as he was, from his injuries. McCain's father looked at the tape and didn't say a word. "His reaction afterward was very emotional, but he never talked...about it. Some things are just too painful for words," McCain writes.

This propaganda photo shows American POWs being given plentiful food, which was not actually the case.

The North Vietnamese were not done using the admiral's son. High-ranking officers visited him in the hospital. Some asked questions. Even General Vo Nguyen Giap, the North Vietnamese minister of defense, who had helped dislodge the French from Vietnam in 1954, came to see McCain. The general looked at the flier and left without saying a word.

One day Bug came to see McCain. He brought with him a tape of a Marine POW criticizing the United States. Bug wanted McCain to make such a tape. He told McCain not to be worried, to speak openly of the war. "I don't feel that way about the war," McCain said, refusing Bug's demand.

Finally, doctors operated on McCain's shattered leg, but with little success. The doctors cut all the ligaments on one side of the knee, which continued to hobble him, as well as his broken arms, for the rest of his life. McCain was still useful as a propaganda tool, even though he was still sickly, running a high fever and suffering from dysentery, a debilitating stomach ailment commonly called diarrhea. McCain had shed 50 pounds. He was down to a paltry 100.

The Voice of Vietnam, the North Vietnam government-run radio outlet, broadcast a commentary titled "From the Pacific to Truc Bach Lake." In the broadcast, the host accused McCain and President Lyndon Johnson of war crimes.

> *In the newest step of war escalation—successive air strikes at Hanoi city these days—Mr. Johnson has wasted scores of U.S aircraft and pilots.*
>
> *Adding to the ever longer list of American pilots captured over North Vietnam was a series of newcomers. John Sidney McCain was one of them. Who is he? A U.S. Navy lieutenant commander…*
>
> *Unfortunately for him, the jet plane he piloted was one of 10 knocked out of Hanoi's sky. He tried in vain to evade the deadly accurate anti-aircraft barrage of fire of this city… the killing he was ordered to do in Vietnam has aroused indignation among the world's peoples…*

What were the feats of arms which McCain achieved? Foreign correspondents in Hanoi saw with their own eyes civilian dwelling houses destroyed and Hanoi's women, old folks and children killed by steel-pellet bombs dropped from McCain's aircraft and those of his colleagues.

McCain was married in 1965 and has a 10-month-old daughter. Surely, he also loves his wife and child. Then why did he fly here dropping bombs on the necks of Vietnamese women and children? What glory had he brought to his father, commander in chief of U.S. Naval Forces in Europe? His grandfather, Adm. John S. McCain, commander of all aircraft carriers in the Pacific in World War II…

But nowadays Lt. Com. McCain is participating in an unjust war, the most unpopular one in U.S. history and mankind's history, too. This is Johnson's war to enslave the Vietnamese People…McCain has brought not reputation for his family in the United States. The one who is smearing McCain's family honor is also smearing the Honor of Washington's United States of America. He is Lyndon B. Johnson.

As the weeks and months went by, McCain's recovery slowed. One night an officer came in and said, "The doctors say that you don't get better. That you get worse."

"You need to put me with some Americans," McCain shot back, "because I'm not going to get any better here."

That night guards placed a blindfold on McCain, put him on a truck and transferred him to a place called the Plantation.

CHAPTER 9

The Plantation

FOR MANY POWS IN VIETNAM, the Air Force pilot Bud Day was a superhero. The North Vietnamese had captured the American flier on August 26, 1967. Day was on a mission to destroy a SAM site about 20 miles inside North Vietnam. Enemy anti-aircraft fire was heavy, and one shell found its way to Day's F-100. Day ejected and parachuted to the ground.

He was badly hurt: He had a black eye and a back injury, and his right arm was broken in three places. Enemy soldiers quickly captured him and placed him in an underground bunker where he remained, tied upside down, for five days. Somehow, despite his injuries, Day loosened his bonds and escaped. It was nothing short of a miracle. He waded into a nearby river, grabbed hold of a bamboo log and used it as a float. Slowly he made his way down the river to South Vietnam, a two-week journey. He crossed the demilitarized zone, or DMZ, an area that separated North and South Vietnam. He wandered through the jungle barefoot, sometimes delirious from lack of food and water. He survived on berries and frogs.

One day as he meandered slowly through the jungle, he heard the *whoop, whoop, whoop* of American helicopters flying overhead. He knew he was close to a U.S. military base. In reality, he was a mile or so from safety, and his hope died as he overheard the chatter of a communist patrol close by. They spotted the escaped flier and shot him in the leg and hand. Day was once again a prisoner of war.

There was no escaping this time. Day's captors took him to the Hanoi Hilton and later to another prison camp called the Zoo. The enemy beat and starved him and threatened to kill him. At one point Day, who would be awarded the Congressional Medal of Honor for his heroic escape and for evading the enemy, arrived at the Plantation. That's where he met and became good friends with a new arrival—John McCain.

★ ★ ★ ★ ★ ★ ★ ★ ★ ★ ★ ★ ★ ★ ★

Medal of Honor Winner

The following is the official citation written when George "Bud" Day received the Congressional Medal of Honor for his heroic escape from the clutches of the North Vietnamese:

On 26 August 1967, Col. Day was forced to eject from his aircraft over North Vietnam when it was hit by ground fire. His right arm was broken in 3 places, and his left knee was badly sprained. He was immediately captured by hostile forces and taken to a prison camp where he was interrogated and severely tortured. After causing the guards to relax their vigilance, Col. Day escaped into the jungle and began the trek toward South Vietnam. Despite injuries inflicted by fragments of a bomb or rocket, he continued southward surviving only on a few berries and uncooked frogs. He successfully evaded enemy patrols and reached the Ben Hai River, where he encountered U.S. artillery barrages. With the aid of a bamboo log float, Col. Day swam across the river and entered the demilitarized zone. Due to delirium, he lost his sense of direction and wandered aimlessly for several days. After several unsuccessful attempts to signal U.S. aircraft, he was ambushed and recaptured by the Viet Cong, sustaining gunshot wounds to his left hand and thigh. He was returned to the prison from which he had escaped and later was moved to Hanoi after giving his captors false information to questions put before him. Physically, Col. Day was totally debilitated and unable to perform even the simplest task for himself. Despite his many injuries, he continued to offer maximum resistance. His personal bravery in the face of deadly enemy pressure was significant in saving the lives of fellow aviators who were still flying against the enemy. Col. Day's conspicuous gallantry and intrepidity at the risk of his life above and beyond the call of duty are in keeping with the highest traditions of the U.S. Air Force and reflect great credit upon himself and the U.S. Armed Forces.

Friendship at Last

Like all of North Vietnam's POW camps, the Plantation, located in northeastern Hanoi, was a hell on earth. Yet it was better than some of the other prison camps, including the notorious Zoo and certainly the infamous Hanoi Hilton, where torture of American servicemen was the order of the day. Photographers staged pictures of POWs at the camp in an attempt to show how "happy" they were and what "wonderful" treatment they got from their North Vietnamese captors.

When Day spotted McCain, the Navy pilot was in rough shape, much rougher than Day, who had his own injuries to mend. McCain's hair and beard had turned white. He was emaciated. Day saw the craggy surgical scar on his knee. McCain's wounded arm was stick-like and unusable. His eyes bugged out. His body was burning with high fever. The North Vietnamese assumed McCain was going to die. They placed the pilot in a cell with Day and another POW, Norris Overly, in an attempt to deny blame if the admiral's son were to succumb.

"I didn't think he was going to live out the day," Day told Robert Timberg.

McCain, however, proved resilient. He slowly started speaking, seemingly happy to be among his countrymen again. His voice was weak and raspy, but the chatter soon ramped up. It got to the point where he wouldn't shut up. "I wouldn't stop talking all through that first day with Bud and Norris," McCain remembers. He told Day and Overly how he was shot down and how the North Vietnamese treated him. He talked about the prison camps and how the communists ran them. He wanted to know how many other Americans were prisoners and where they were held.

Day and Overly both knew who McCain's father was. They felt a special bond with the Navy aviator. "As the day went on . . . I started to get the feeling that if we could get a little grits into him and feed him and get him cleaned up and the infection didn't get him, he was probably going to make it," said Day. "And that surprised me. That just flabbergasted me because I had given him up."

That night Day realized something about McCain: "this guy's got a lot of heart. You've been involved in sports and games and things where people kind of rise to an occasion, and that was him. He was rising. And if he hadn't been, he'd have been dead. If he had not had that will to live and that determination, he'd have been dead."

Coming Back

Slowly, day by day, hour by hour, Bud Day and Norris Overly put the broken pieces of John McCain back together. They washed him as best as they could, a struggle because his body was caked with dirt, grime and crud from the weeks of living in abhorrent conditions. Overly massaged McCain's legs at least two hours a day. They helped him eat and drink.

By the fifth day after his arrival, the encrusted dirt on McCain's face began to flake off. After a time, McCain could shave. His spirits began to rise. He began feeling human again. The constant cleansing of his injured leg with soap and water started to reduce the infection. By January 1968, 15 months after he was shot down, McCain was making progress. He was using makeshift crutches to take small steps, something he hadn't done since his arrival in North Vietnam. Once he got up and started taking those first tentative steps, McCain felt the power come back to his shattered body. "Soon I was able to stand unaided, and even maneuver around my cell on a pair of crutches."

McCain's spirits soared, too. Being in the company of Americans, his fellow soldiers, brought him comfort and hope. "I was frail, but voluble.

Bud and Norris accommodated me to the best of their ability, and were the soul of kindness as they eased my way to what they believed was my imminent death," McCain said.

McCain spoke to Day extensively about his confinement. The Navy aviator was in awe of the Air Force pilot and the way he endured brutal torture. "His captors had looped rope around his shoulders, tightened it until his shoulders were nearly touching and then hung him by the arms from the rafters of the torture room, tearing his shoulders apart. Left in this condition for hours, Bud never acceded to the Vietnamese demands for military information. They had to re-fracture his broken right arm and threaten to break the other before Bud gave them anything at all…he was a tough man, a fierce resister, whose example was an inspiration to every man who served with him."

McCain slept a lot during those first few weeks at the Plantation, sometimes 20 hours a day. Each day that he was alive was a gift. He grew stronger.

The Corn Crib

In early January, guards moved McCain and the others to another part of the prison camp called the Corn Crib. McCain and Day stayed together. On each side of McCain's cell were more Americans. It was tough to communicate with the others, but the POWs managed ingenious, albeit crude ways to stay in contact. Sometimes they would yell whenever guards were not around. They left notes written in cigarette ash in a washroom drain.

The North Vietnamese interrogators still pursued information, though not as robustly as their counterparts at the Hanoi Hilton. Still, they wanted

McCain and the other POWs to denounce the war and President Johnson. The Americans refused. McCain fought back the only way he could—with his words. When a group of North Vietnamese dignitaries visited his cell, McCain did not hold back.

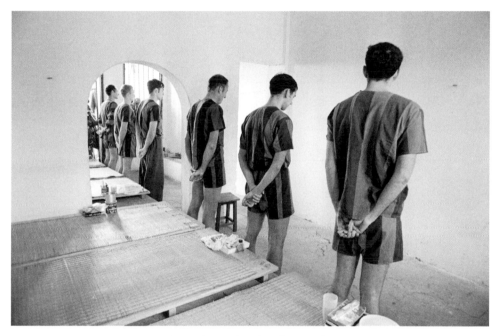

American POWs, cleaned up by the North Vietnamese,
await their release to the United States.

Lt. Colonel Jack Van Loan, a POW imprisoned with McCain, witnessed the event. He told Robert Timberg, "John was just fighting back as best as he knew how. I was crying and laughing at the same time. Here's a guy that's all crippled up, all busted up, and he doesn't know if he's going to live to the next day, and literally blew them out of there with a verbal assault. You can't imagine the example John set for the rest of the camp by doing that."

As time went on, some conditions in the prison improved. McCain and the others were getting enough to eat. They even had their fill of bananas for a few days. The questioning stopped for a time. "Once we were instructed to write summaries of our military histories. We invented all the details," McCain said. "Mine contained references to service in Antarctica and as a naval attaché in Oslo."

No one knew what the North Vietnamese were up to. Why did they want the information? The POWs also saw that officials were questioning Overly. The prisoners quickly surmised the enemy wanted to determine whether Overly was suitable to be released in a sort of "amnesty" that would make the North Vietnamese look good in the eyes of the world. Bud Day advised Overly to turn down the offer. The Code of Conduct for prisoners was clear: A POW had to refuse release until those who had been captured earlier had left.

Overly left anyway. On February 16, McCain, carried on a stretcher, and Day were taken to say goodbye to Overly. A camera crew filmed the event. Overly told Day he had not made any propaganda statements for the North Vietnamese. Two other prisoners also took early release. Some of the POWs looked down on these men.

McCain had a different view. "Norris had taken good care of me. He saved my life. I thought him a good man then, as I do today. I feared he had made a mistake, but I couldn't stand in judgment of him. I thought too well of him, and owed him too much to stand between him and freedom. I wished him well as he departed, carrying a letter from me to Carol in his pocket."

When spring bloomed in 1968, guards removed Bud Day from the cell he shared with McCain. Guards had seen how well McCain was getting around on his crude crutches. They took Day to another prison camp and moved McCain to the largest cellblock at the Plantation—called the Warehouse. The admiral's son was now in solitary confinement and would stay there for two years.

★ ★ ★ ★ ★ ★ ★ ★ ★ ★ ★ ★ ★ ★ ★ ★

POW Camps in North Vietnam

The North Vietnamese had a total of 12 permanent prisoner of war camps that held U.S. soldiers and airmen, and a number of other temporary camps and detention centers that the communists built to detain and house those they had captured. Although most of the prison camps did not have official names, the Americans gave each one a particular moniker.

For example, there was Alcatraz, located in north central Hanoi, which opened in 1967. Alcatraz, named after the island in San Francisco Bay where a federal prison stood, was a small jail located on the grounds of the Ministry of Defense. There was also Camp Faith, which became operational in 1970 as the North started to put all its U.S. prisoners into one place. It was at Camp Faith, located about 10 miles west of Hanoi, where the North Vietnamese allowed prisoners to mingle with each another.

Then, of course, there was the Hanoi Hilton, officially called the Hoa Lo Prison. Located in downtown Hanoi, it served as the processing point for captured U.S. servicemen. Hoa Lo was the most notorious of the North Vietnamese prison camps. Built by the

French early in the 20th century, the prison was a house of torture, brutality and death. When the time came, the camp also became the place where POWs gathered for their release back to the United States.

CHAPTER 10

The Torture of Solitary

IT IS ALMOST IMPOSSIBLE for the average person to understand the terror and pain American prisoners of war suffered at the hands of their North Vietnamese captors. In 2015, Sam Johnson, a U.S. congressman and Vietnam veteran, tried to explain in an article for the online news magazine *Politico* what it was like to be an American POW in Vietnam. Johnson wasn't a novice Air Force pilot. Vietnam was his second war. He flew 62 combat missions during the Korean War and 25 during Vietnam. His 25th mission was his last.

Johnson was 35 years old when he and his co-pilot were shot down over North Vietnam during what was supposed to be a simple mission to destroy an enemy anti-aircraft battery and a truck depot. Johnson was piloting his craft low along the tree line, or on "the deck."

The enemy fired. Johnson fired back. But his plane's guns jammed. Enemy bullets ripped through the engine of his now defenseless F-4 Phantom. Johnson and his co-pilot ejected just before the plane crashed. They landed right in the lap of the enemy. The soldiers took the father of three to the Hoa Lo Prison, the Hanoi Hilton.

Johnson spent almost seven years in captivity at Hoa Lo, an experience that shaped the way he would live the rest of his life. "I learned firsthand that the trying times do have a purpose and that we must choose to let them make us stronger. We must choose to keep a positive attitude. And sometimes we have to make that choice many times throughout the day," Johnson writes.

Nothing prepared Johnson for Hoa Lo. Prisoners were routinely tied up and attached with ropes to a hook that hung from the ceiling. "This would go on for hours, sometimes even days on end. Aside from leg irons and leg stocks—both of which were used on me for months and years on end—[this] was a favorite instrument of torture at the Hanoi Hilton. I was spared the device only because I was already so injured. Some of my friends, however, were not so lucky."

U.S. Congressman Sam Johnson, a former POW, at the dedication of the Texas Vietnam Veterans Memorial in Austin.

Alone

Like Johnson, John McCain had been beaten and tortured to within an inch of his young life at the Hanoi Hilton. Now McCain faced a different kind of torture—solitary confinement. It was as painful as the physical injuries he had suffered at the hands of his captors.

After McCain and Bud Day were split up at the Plantation, the Vietnamese placed McCain in a cell by himself. He, like the other POWs at the Plantation, had no contact with anyone except an occasional guard. Physical beatings were one thing, but the mental anguish of being alone was something McCain was not prepared for.

"It's an awful thing, solitary," McCain writes. "It crushes your spirit and weakens your resistance more effectively than any other form of mistreatment. Having no one else to rely on, to share confidences with, to seek counsel from, you begin to doubt your judgment and your courage. But you eventually adjust to solitary, as you can to almost any hardship, by devising various methods to keep your mind off your troubles and greedily grasping any opportunity for human contact."

Despair hung over McCain like a black cloud during the first few weeks of his lonely, mind-numbing confinement. He devised mental tricks and games to keep his mind active. He tried desperately to memorize the names of other POWs and the guards who lorded over them. He went over the names of all the pilots in his squadron and the other squadrons aboard the *Oriskany*. "I also prayed more often and more fervently than I ever had as a free man."

As McCain sat in the dark dungeon of his mind, he lamented that he hadn't read more books. Reading more, he mused later in his autobiography, would have helped him keep his mind sharp, his thoughts focused. He had time, lots of time, to remember the past. He began to feel ashamed for the "foolishness that had characterized my youth."

"I had my normal share of regrets, but regret for choosing the career that had landed me in this place was not among them."

★ ★ ★ ★ ★ ★ ★ ★ ★ ★ ★ ★ ★ ★ ★

Coping Skills

During the Vietnam War, 662 U.S. soldiers, sailors and airmen survived captivity and were later released. Of these, 94 were released from the beginning of the war until 1973. In the spring of that year, the North Vietnamese set 568 men free as part of Operation Homecoming.

In 1977, San Diego State University, along with the Center for Prisoner of War Studies at the Naval Health Research Center, conducted a study of how specific "time-killing" activities and other "adaptive behaviors" helped prisoners cope with long periods spent in solitary confinement.

The study, which included a series of questions that 137 former POWs, all Navy aviators, answered, concluded that "reliving the past" was a good coping mechanism during the first few weeks. The study's authors also said that using other coping techniques over a longer period, such as repetitive mental exercises or "self-development" activities, such as McCain writing a play in his head, were extremely useful.

Battling Back

It was important for a POW's sanity and self-respect to fight back as well as he could. Each soldier fought his battle in a different way. Some POWs spent hours going over a particular hobby in their head. Others tried to remember the specifics of a college course they had once taken. Some worked out complicated math equations in their heads or the design of a building or an airplane. McCain authored books and plays in his head. He even acted scenes of those plays in the darkness and solitude of his miserable cell.

"On several occasions, I became terribly annoyed when a guard entered my cell to take me to the bath or to bring me food and disrupted some flight of fantasy where the imagined comforts were so attractive that I could not easily bear to be deprived of them," he writes.

In the isolation of captivity, there is a thin line between reality and fantasy. Some POWs crossed that line and never came back. "Sadly, I knew of a few men in prison who had grown so content with their imaginary worlds that they preferred solitary confinement and turned down the offer of a roommate. Eventually, they stopped communicating with the rest of us."

Boredom and Hanoi Hannah

The Plantation was once a wonderful example of French colonial architecture. Located in Hanoi, the estate, where the city's former mayor and family lived, was adorned with gardens and trees. By the time it was converted into a prison, the Plantation's colonial charm had crumbled away. The Americans called it the "Big House."

All the prisoners at the Big House had their own cell and rarely saw the light of the day. The windows of each cubicle were boarded up to prevent the POWs from communicating with one another. Only small holes near the top of the wall provided wisps of ventilation.

Every door had a small opening, a peephole, that the guards could look through from the outside. The only way McCain could see whether it was raining, or if the sun was shining, or what his guards were up to, was through this tiny slit in his cell door. For hours McCain would peer through the crack, hoping to witness some activity, such as a guard tripping while walking by or other POWs being taken in for questioning.

The daily routine was dull. It began at six in the morning when a gong echoed across the camp. Each new day of monotony and tedium began with a half hour of Hanoi Hannah, the "Voice of Vietnam," broadcast through loudspeakers across the camp.

Hanoi Hannah's real name was Trinh Thi Ngo. It was the GIs (a slang abbreviation for American soldiers) who nicknamed her. North Vietnam's Defense Ministry wrote all her scripts in the hopes of sapping the Americans of their morale and convincing them they were fighting an unjust war. "Defect, GI," Hanoi Hannah once urged. "It is a very good idea to leave a sinking ship. You know you cannot win this war."

The radio broadcast was a propaganda tool and, according to McCain, "a pretty good source of entertainment." Although Hanoi Hannah berated the Americans for fighting an "illegal war," she brought them news from the United States. She highlighted anti-war protests and rioting in some cities. Once in 1969, she mistakenly told the POWs that an American astronaut had become the first human to set foot on the moon. The story was upbeat and made the Americans cheer.

Trinh Thi Ngo, also known as Hanoi Hannah, in 1995.

Hanoi Hannah also played recordings of anti-war speeches in the United States. She regaled listeners with patriotic Vietnamese songs and a few American tunes from vinyl records that the French had left behind.

When the broadcast was over (it was taped from the night before), the guards opened each cell door. The POWs were directed to set their waste buckets on the ground. They were then forced back inside their lonely hovels. The guards locked the doors again. Within a few minutes, two prisoners walked by and picked up the buckets, brimming with human waste, and emptied the containers in a large pit at the back of the camp. POWs washed the buckets and returned them to each cell. Often, the men found ways to pass messages, written on scraps of paper, when the buckets were returned.

Once the bucket brigade had finished, the guards filled up the prisoners' teapots. Winter was the rainy season in Vietnam so the prisoners washed twice a week because there was plenty of water. During the dry summer, the prisoners seldom washed. Breakfast was usually a piece of bread and a bowl of some type of vegetable broth. The small amount of food allotted to each prisoner tasted awful. The guards ate the same food and didn't seem to care. They were undisciplined soldiers who fared slightly better and were just a bit cleaner than the POWs.

All activity, such as it was, stopped after breakfast. Between meals, prisoners had nothing to do. They were given no mental or physical stimulation. There was nothing to read, save the occasional piece of communist propaganda literature. The next round of "excitement" came at lunchtime. At noon, the guards sounded the gong again. It was time to take a two-hour nap.

Living such a lonely, mind-numbing routine made McCain surly and depressed. It also caused him a great deal of pain. A vicious cycle ensued. Still, McCain began to improve. The dysentery subsided and he was able to keep food down. He regained his strength and start limping around in his cell, though it took longer to recoup the power in his battered arms. Once he attempted a push-up. He made it down to the ground but lacked the strength to push back up.

Along with his improving physical strength came mental strength. He fought back the only way he could—shouting insults at the guards, "resorting to the belligerence that I had relied on earlier in my life when obliged to suffer one indignity or another." He was uncooperative. His "bad behavior," however, boosted his spirits.

The guards responded to his insults by beating him. One guard, tired of McCain's diatribe, came into his cell and kicked McCain as he lay on the floor. McCain, however, was undeterred and kept shouting. The guard knew McCain's right leg was injured, so he stomped on it. The pain ripped through McCain's body like a sharp knife. Sometimes the guard kicked him in the head, but never in the face. This led McCain to believe that the guards were under orders to "go easy" on him because of his pedigree as an admiral's son.

The physical torture was one thing. The pain would eventually subside. Yet the mental torment continued. With so much time alone, a person becomes hyperaware of his pain. McCain was still suffering pain from his injuries and it sometimes felt unbearable.

The prison medic, a man the POWs called "Zorba," visited only three or four times a year. He'd look McCain over and simply tell him to eat and exercise more. It was a bizarre prescription. McCain became his own doctor, which made him angrier and more pessimistic about surviving this inhuman ordeal.

Tap, Tap, Tap

The POWs were clever individuals. Although silence was the order of the day, they devised different ways to communicate. If the Vietnamese figured out one method, however, they quickly put a stop to it, forcing the prisoners to resort to other communication systems. For example, when the guards moved the POWs from one area to another, the prisoners used their hands to signal the other POWs peering through the slits in their doors. The POWs also developed a complicated but highly effective code-tapping system. If a prisoner wanted to chat, he'd tap out the old song lyric "shave and a haircut," each knock corresponding to a syllable in the phrase. The response by the other prisoner was "two bits." They devised a system where each series of taps on a wall meant a different letter. The prisoners listened to these taps, which allowed them to spell out words.

"We divided the alphabet into five columns of five letters each," McCain remembers. "The letter K was dropped. A, F, L, Q, and V were the key letters. Tap once for the five letters in the A column, twice for F, three times for L, and so on. After indicating the column, pause for a beat, then tap one through five times and it indicated the right letter."

Another way the prisoners communicated was to place their enamel drinking cups against the concrete wall of their cell. The POWs wrapped a shirt around the cup and spoke softly through it, which enabled the person in the adjacent cell to hear.

Whether tapping, talking through a shirt and a cup or writing bits of messages on scraps of paper, McCain and the others talked about themselves. When a new prisoner arrived, he was a treasure trove of new information. The POWs tried desperately to get as much news from him as possible.

CHAPTER 11

"Do You Want to Go Home?"

IN THE EARLY SUMMER OF 1968, after almost a year of imprisonment, John McCain finally figured out why he always thought the North Vietnamese were giving him special treatment. One evening in June, McCain's routine abruptly changed. Previously, each time the North Vietnamese interrogated McCain, the ritual was the same. Guards would take McCain out of his cell and take him to an empty room, dank with moisture and mold. McCain was ordered to sit on a stool, while his interrogator sat behind a desk.

The interviewer would ask McCain the usual questions. And as usual, McCain refused to cooperate or answer, which came as no surprise to the Vietnamese officer. The interrogator then told McCain that he'd never go home again and he'd be put on trial as a war criminal. It was the same game played time after time.

But on this summer night in 1968, the pattern changed. Instead of being questioned in a sparse cell, the guards took McCain into another room. This one was bigger, more luxurious. It had plush chairs and a glass coffee table topped with a plate of cookies, a pot of tea, and cigarettes. The usual interrogator was nowhere to be found. Instead, in the room that day was Major Bai, whom the POWs called Cat. McCain remembered him well: He was the man who had been so dissatisfied with McCain's answers during Chalais' interview at the hospital.

Cat was the head of all the prisoner of war camps in Hanoi. He was a brutal man who had no ethical qualms about torturing POWs. Also in the room was an interpreter, whom the GIs called Rabbit.

McCain took a seat, a bit bewildered at the change of venue and the gifts laid out on the table. Cat started the conversation as calmly as if the two had met at a café in Paris. Cat said that he had run the prison camps during the French Indochina War between 1945 and 1954. Cat remarked that he occasionally set some prisoners free. He then shifted the conversation to McCain's father, his family and the war in general.

For two rambling hours, Cat talked and McCain listened, sometimes commenting, other times not. Finally, the major stared McCain in the eye and got to the point. Did he know that his friend Norris Overly and the other prisoners the North Vietnamese had sent home had been welcomed back in the United States as heroes?

McCain was unfazed. "That's interesting," he said simply.

Then Cat asked a question McCain didn't expect: "Do you want to be released?"

McCain was dumbfounded. Had he heard Major Bai right? Did Bai just ask if he wanted to go home? The room was silent. Finally, the weight of the query settled in. McCain didn't know how to answer.

"I was astonished by the offer and didn't immediately know how to respond," McCain writes. "I wasn't in great shape, was still considerably underweight and miserable with dysentery and heat rash. The prospect of going home to my family was powerfully tempting."

American POWS are marched before a joint
military commission for interviews.

But McCain was a Navy officer, a graduate of Annapolis. He knew
his duty. He knew his job. More importantly, he knew what the Code of
Conduct for prisoners of war said about such things. McCain also knew
there would be a price to pay if he accepted.

"The Vietnamese usually required prisoners who were released early
to make some statement that indicated their gratitude or at least their
desire to be released," McCain writes. "They viewed such expressions as
assurances that the released prisoner would not denounce his captors

once he was back home, and spoil whatever propaganda value his release was intended to serve. Accordingly, they would not force a prisoner to go home."

McCain thought about Cat's offer, yet refused to commit himself.

"Go back and think about it," Cat urged.

McCain went back to his cell and had a long talk with himself. Answers did not come easy. McCain decided he needed help and guidance. Seeing his wife and kids again was a strong incentive to say yes. But what about his comrades in arms? What would they think, do and say if the son of an admiral simply got up and walked out the prison gates? It was a moral quagmire, a dilemma that pained McCain greatly.

McCain decided to tap on the wall, hoping to rouse his neighbor Bob Craner. McCain wanted another American's opinion. He needed to sound Craner out. As he tapped his messages in the secret code of the Plantation POWs, McCain thought about another young Navy flier who had already spent four years as a prisoner of war.

Everett Alvarez Jr.

Everett Alvarez was a child of the Depression, an economic calamity that had tossed the United States into a social and financial maelstrom during the 1930s. He was the son of Mexican immigrants who had married at a very young age. The couple settled in the verdant fields of Salinas, California, and made a home. Alvarez was the first in his family to graduate from high school. He later joined the Navy and began flight training in Pensacola and in Texas. He reported for duty aboard the aircraft carrier USS *Constellation*.

In the spring of 1964, the *Constellation* steamed into the South China Sea and positioned itself at Yankee Station. From the carrier, Alvarez flew reconnaissance missions over the Ho Chi Minh Trail, a supply route through Laos and Cambodia that the communists used to bring guns, ammunition, soldiers and food down from North Vietnam to South Vietnam.

On August 4, North Vietnamese torpedo boats attacked the USS *Maddox*, a destroyer patrolling in the Gulf of Tonkin. After the Gulf of Tonkin incident, as historians would later call it, Congress gave President Johnson a "blank check" to pursue increased military action in Indochina.

The next day, the president ordered a retaliatory strike against North Vietnam. Alvarez was part of that mission. He took off from the deck of the *Constellation* and flew his Skyhawk across the gulf, dodging the heavy anti-aircraft flak that darkened the daytime sky. Alvarez dropped his bombs on several enemy docks.

"On my first pass, I fired all my rockets," Alvarez remembered years later in an interview published on History.Net. "Then I was low to ground. Coming on my second pass, I flipped on my 20mm guns and made a strafing pass, blasting the torpedo boats.... As I leveled my wings to head out to sea, we had to cross a spit of land at treetop level. Then I hear this big 'poof'—I'm hit. I immediately lost control of the plane.... I said, 'I'm hit, I'm getting out, guys!'"

Alvarez ejected at a low altitude and came down in the gulf. He was only slightly injured, but in big trouble. The North Vietnamese immediately captured him. He became the first American pilot to be taken prisoner. The enemy took Alvarez to the Hanoi Hilton, where he was beaten, tortured and interrogated for years.

Lt. Everett Alvarez in a photograph before he
was taken prisoner by the North Vietnamese.

"Suddenly I was thrown into this medieval environment and kept thinking, 'God, why me?'" Alvarez told a reporter for *People* magazine. "I fully expected the door to open and someone to say he was here to take me home. But as the days went by, I didn't know how much longer it would be." He'd be one of the first released in 1973.

Advice

Craner heard McCain's taps. The two had never actually seen each other, which meant Craner didn't know just how bad McCain's physical shape was. Craner had only heard through the prison grapevine that McCain's health was not good. The two "talked" as well as they could through the concrete wall between their cells.

McCain told Craner about the Cat's offer and that he didn't think he should go home before Alvarez. McCain also believed he would be violating the Code of Conduct. Craner was unmoved. He told McCain he would not be in violation of the Code if he accepted. "You don't know if you can survive this," Craner told McCain. "The seriously injured can go home."

McCain proved stubborn. "I think I can make it," he said. "The Vietnamese tell me I won't, but if they really thought that I'm in such bad shape they would have at least sent a doctor around to check on me."

"What do they want from you in return?" Craner asked.

"They didn't say," McCain answered.

"Well, when you go back, just play along with them. See what they want to let you go. If it's not much, take it."

McCain balked. He "didn't want to go down that road." It would turn into a "slippery slope" if he started negotiating with the enemy. Besides, Everett Alvarez and a lot of others should go home first.

Deep down, McCain wanted out. Who wouldn't? His nearly two years in captivity had sapped his energy, left him nearly crippled and caused emotional and mental anguish. Yet he couldn't think only of himself.

"Moreover, I knew that every prisoner the Vietnamese tried to break, those who had arrived before me and those who would come after me, would be taunted with the story of how an admiral's son had gone home early, a lucky beneficiary of America's class-conscious society. I knew that my release would add to the suffering of men who were already straining to keep faith with their country. I was injured, but I believed I could survive. I couldn't persuade myself to leave."

The conversation of taps continued. Craner insisted McCain take the offer. McCain was hesitant, noting the propaganda victory the Vietnamese would win if he caved. He told Craner he didn't want to be disloyal.

Decision Time

McCain had gotten the advice he sought. As he sat in his cell thinking about what to do, he realized that although he would not take Craner's advice, it had helped him clarify his own position. Several days later, he again faced Cat. "What is your answer?" the major asked.

"No, thank you."

"Why?" Cat wanted to know.

McCain explained the Code of Conduct. He told his captor that POWs could not accept amnesty, special favors or parole. He said that Everett Alvarez, who was still in captivity, should go home first.

Cat then explained the obvious: You, Cat told McCain, are in terrible physical condition. McCain agreed, but said he'd make it through captivity.

"President Johnson has ordered you home," Cat then bellowed.

"Show me the orders," McCain brusquely responded. "Show me the orders, and I'll believe you."

Cat knew how to manipulate people. That was his job. He pulled out a letter supposedly from Carol, McCain's wife. The letter said she was saddened her husband had not been released with Norris and the others. McCain knew better, though. He knew Carol would not write such a letter. She would not have wanted her husband to dishonor himself. Cat grew impatient. He dismissed McCain and gave him the letter to take back to his cell.

A week later the two men talked again. This time McCain was weak from his ever-present battle with dysentery. McCain cut the interview short because he felt ill. Cat was angry. He thought McCain was rude.

"Now It Will Be Very Bad for You"

Cat wanted McCain out. His release would be a huge coup for North Vietnam. But Cat wasn't about to forcibly expel him. Instead, the major promised that McCain did not have to make any propaganda statements. McCain knew in his heart that the major was lying. If the flier accepted, the Vietnamese would pressure him to record a statement.

On July 4, one of the officers entered McCain's cell and said he knew of the offer. "You will have a nice family reunion, Mac Kane," the officer said in a heavy Vietnamese accent. McCain agreed with that assessment, but once again said he was not going to accept. A few hours later, Cat and

McCain met yet again. This time there were no cookies, tea, cigarettes or plush chairs. The meeting took place in a regular interrogation room. Cat was fuming. He told McCain to sit on the stool. He again made the offer to McCain through Rabbit, the interpreter.

"Our senior officer wants to know your final answer," Rabbit said.

"My final answer is no."

Cat was so furious he broke a pen he was holding. The ink flew onto a newspaper on the desk. Cat kicked a chair, then yelled, "They taught you too well, Mac Kane. They taught you too well." Cat stormed out of the room.

Rabbit stayed behind. He looked at "Mac Kane."

"Now it will be very bad for you, Mac Kane," Rabbit said. "Go back to your room."

McCain sighed heavily. "I knew a bad time lay ahead, and that I would soon confront a greater measure of my enemy's cruelty, an experience many of my comrades had already endured but I had been spared," McCain writes. "I had seen the Cat's fury, and it had made a deep impression on me. I tried to be fatalistic, and prepare myself to suffer the inevitable without dishonoring myself."

John McCain had no idea of what Cat had in store for him. His desire to adhere to his strong belief in a soldier's code of conduct, however, was stronger than his fear. McCain's strength would be tested many times over after this incident with Cat. But he would prove victorious. Inevitably, these episodes would prepare him for different kind of battle later in his life. They would not be physical tests, but McCain's honor and ethics would be tested and he would not disappoint.

★ ★ ★ ★ ★ ★ ★ ★ ★ ★ ★ ★ ★ ★ ★

Code of the U.S. Fighting Force

After the Korean War ended in 1953, the U.S. military established the Code of Conduct for soldiers who were taken prisoner by the enemy. At that time, the country was shocked when several POWs refused to return to the United States, choosing instead to live in China. Soon, reports began to leak out about POWs who had mistreated other prisoners while in captivity. The U.S. government took many former prisoners to court over a variety of offenses, including desertion to the enemy and treason.

Concerned military leaders then established the Code of Conduct for POWs. The Code informed soldiers what was expected of them if they were captured. President Dwight D. Eisenhower signed the Code of Conduct into law in 1955. It has been changed twice, the last time in 1988. It has six provisions:

Article I

I am an American, fighting in the forces which guard my country and our way of life. I am prepared to give my life in their defense.

Article II

I will never surrender of my own free will. If in command, I will never surrender the members of my command while they still have the means to resist.

Article III

If I am captured I will continue to resist by all means available. I will make every effort to escape and to aid others to escape. I will accept neither parole nor special favors from the enemy.

Article IV

If I become a prisoner of war, I will keep faith with my fellow prisoners. I will give no information or take part in any action which might be harmful to my comrades. If I am senior, I will take command. If not, I will obey the lawful orders of those appointed over me and will back them up in every way.

Article V

When questioned, should I become a prisoner of war, I am required to give name, rank, service number, and date of birth. I will evade answering further questions to the utmost of my ability. I will make no oral or written statements disloyal to my country and its allies or harmful to their cause.

Article VI

I will never forget that I am an American, fighting for freedom, responsible for my actions, and dedicated to the principles which made my country free. I will trust in my God and in the United States of America.

CHAPTER 12

Dark Days

FOR A MONTH, John McCain waited to feel the wrath Cat planned to unleash. It finally came one night in late August. A guard took McCain to a large room. Waiting inside was the prison camp's commander and an interpreter. Cat had been frustrated by McCain once before. Not again. The camp commander would do Cat's dirty work this time. As McCain looked around, he realized that it was the same room the POWs had used the year before for Christmas services.

The commander eyed the bedraggled McCain and accused him of committing "black crimes against the people." He also unleashed a torrent of accusations, blaming McCain for breaking many of the camp rules. It was time, the commander roared, that McCain confess his crimes.

McCain, never one to back down from a confrontation, replied with a vulgar phrase.

"Why do you treat your guards disrespectfully?" the commander asked through the interpreter.

"Because they treat me like an animal," McCain shot back.

In the room stood several guards. The commander said something in Vietnamese that McCain did not understand. The soldiers grabbed

McCain and started punching, kicking and stomping his already battered body. McCain crumpled to the floor, bleeding.

"Are you ready to confess your crimes?" the commander asked again.

McCain said no.

The commander then signaled the guards. They picked McCain up from the floor and sat him on a stool. They tied a rope around his arms and secured it behind his back. The soldiers left the room and McCain spent the rest of the night bound to the wobbly perch.

"In the morning," McCain writes, "three guards came in, removed the rope, and took me to an interrogation room, where the deputy commander, a dull-witted man we called Frankenstein for his bulging forehead and numerous facial warts, waited for me."

Frankenstein, as his commander had done the previous day, ordered McCain to confess to war crimes.

Again, McCain refused.

This time the guards dragged McCain to a room behind his cell. The room was empty except for a waste bucket. There was no door, only a single window covered by shutters large enough for a person to pass through. They dumped McCain in the room and left him for four horrifying days. Guards visited McCain every two or three hours and beat him mercilessly. Some of them enjoyed inflicting pain on a helpless man and did it with grim vigor. Others were not as committed and administered a minimal punishment. Usually one guard held McCain while the other two beat him.

When McCain fell to the floor, he felt the pain of boots kicking his body and ramming into his head. His torturers broke his ribs and knocked out some teeth. The beatings reinjured his already damaged right knee.

When the guards were finished, McCain was left to wallow in his own blood and waste. As one day turned into two and then three, McCain's desire to fight back slowly began to leave him. The beatings began to blend one into another. They broke his body, and then, finally, they broke John McCain's spirit. He had no more fight left. The arrogance and belligerence that had sustained him these past eight months were gone.

A Defiant Decision

The pain that racked his body was unbearable. The mental torture was immense. McCain wanted it to end. He yearned to be free of the horror his life had become. But how? The answer was clear. He could not lie down for the North Vietnamese. He would not besmirch his character as a member of the U.S. Armed Forces. McCain took a long shot. He would attempt to take his own life, an act of defiance that would deny the North Vietnamese the satisfaction of killing him.

"I doubt I really intended to kill myself," he writes. "But I couldn't fight anymore, and I remember deciding that the last thing I could do to make them believe I was still resisting, that I wouldn't break, was to attempt suicide."

Somehow McCain mustered the energy to stand. He stood his broken body on the waste bucket near the window and braced himself against the wall.

He laced his filthy prison-issue shirt through the window's shutters and strung it around his neck. Outside one of the guards saw what McCain was doing. He rushed in and pulled McCain from the window, saving his life, as he had hoped someone would. He saw soon after, however, that his plan had not worked. He knew the beatings would continue.

On the fourth day, McCain writes, "I gave up."

He decided to confess. He informed his captors.

An interrogator took out a sheet of paper and began writing: "I am a black criminal, and I have performed the deeds of an air pirate. I almost died and the Vietnamese people saved my life. The doctors gave me an operation that I did not deserve."

The guards then ordered him to write out the confession in his own hand. It took half a day and many drafts. McCain wanted to make it obvious that he had been forced to sign it, rather than doing so of his own free will.

A photograph taken at a detention center in Hanoi shows a POW talking to fellow prisoners through barred windows in March 1973. Operation Homecoming had commenced, bringing more than 500 American soldiers home.

The interrogator read McCain's final effort, then rewrote it once again. He returned it to McCain and again told him to copy it in his own handwriting. Somehow, the stubborn arrogance that had characterized John McCain throughout his life reared up again. He refused to rewrite the draft. More argument ensued and the two fought about what the confession should say. Finally, McCain, tired, worn and hurt, having staged his "last stand" at defiance, gave in.

Ashamed

As a tidal wave of shame washed over McCain, he felt himself weak and alone. In his mind, the enemy had won. What McCain didn't know was that he wasn't alone. Nearly every American POW who had refused to cooperate with the Vietnamese had suffered the same agonizing fate. Each had tried to resist in his own way. Navy commander James Stockdale, who had been shot down in September 1965 and would later receive the Medal of Honor for his conduct while a POW, beat his own face with a stool rather than confess. In the end, he signed. Another pilot, Jeremiah Denton, confessed too. As his confession was filmed, Denton blinked t-o-r-t-u-r-e in Morse code so viewers would know he was confessing under extreme pressure and duress.

"I was ashamed," McCain writes. "I felt faithless, and couldn't control my despair. I shook, as if my disgrace were a fever. I kept imagining my pride was lost, and I doubted I would ever stand up to any man again. Nothing could save me. No one would ever look upon me again with anything but pity or contempt."

But a written confession was not enough. The Vietnamese wanted McCain to record it on tape, which he reluctantly did. He confessed to his "crimes against the Vietnamese people."

"I, as a U.S. airman, am guilty of crimes against the Vietnamese country and people. I bombed their cities, towns and villages and caused many injuries, even deaths, for the people of Vietnam," McCain said on the tape, which was broadcast on radio across North and South Vietnam. "I was captured in the capital city of Hanoi, while attacking it. After I was captured, I was taken to the hospital in Hanoi, where I received very good medical treatment. I was given an operation on my leg, which allowed me to walk again, and a cast on my right arm, which was badly broken in three places.

"The doctors were very good and they knew a great deal about the practice of medicine. I remained in the hospital for some time and regained much of my health and strength. Since I arrived in the camp of detention, I received humane and lenient treatment.

"I received this kind treatment and food even though I came here as an aggressor and the people who I injured have much difficulty in their living standards. I wish to express my deep gratitude for my kind treatment and I will never forget this kindness extended to me."

On June 6, 1969, United Press International reported McCain's confession. "The English-language broadcast monitored in Saigon was one of a recent series from American prisoners in North Vietnam beamed into South Vietnam by Radio Hanoi," the dispatch read. "The series apparently was initiated in response to [U.S.] Defense Secretary Melvin Laird's May 19 statement that there were 'serious questions' about whether U.S. prisoners were receiving humane treatment."

The End of Isolation

The year 1968 passed into 1969, which turned into 1970, and McCain was still a captive. The days seemed to grow longer. There were many times when he and the other POWs felt as if God had abandoned them. They felt alone.

"Hungry, beaten, hurt, scared, and alone, human beings can begin to feel that they are removed from God's love," McCain writes. "The anguish can lead to resentment, to the awful despair that God has forsaken you."

Still, McCain was able to reach down and find faith in himself as well as in God. He began to look at his suffering in biblical terms. He compared himself and his comrades to Job, who suffered greatly but was ultimately rewarded by God.

For the most part, the beatings ended for McCain and the others by the end of 1969. He had been moved back to the Hanoi Hilton in late December of that year. Finally in 1970, McCain's isolation ended as well. That year, the North Vietnamese moved him to a room that housed many POWs. They called the area Camp Unity. It had seven cell blocks with 30 to 40 prisoners inside. At Camp Unity, McCain saw many of his old friends, including Bob Craner and Bud Day.

"If you have never been deprived of liberty in solitude, you cannot know what ineffable joy you experience in the open company of other human beings, free to talk and joke without fear," McCain remembers. "The strength you acquire in fraternity with others who share your fate is immeasurable."

That first night in Camp Unity, not a single soldier slept. They shared their experiences. What did this all mean? Were they going home? "We talked about news from home. We talked about our families, and the lives we hoped to return to soon…. I have lived many happy years since, and am a blessed and contented man. But I will never experience again the supreme happiness I felt my fourth Christmas in Hanoi."

Operation Homecoming

In April 1972, with the ground war continuing unabated and POWs still in North Vietnam, President Richard Nixon (who had taken office in 1969) resumed the bombing campaign known as Operation Rolling Thunder. (President Johnson had halted the bombing operation in 1968.) The reason for renewing the strike was to force the North Vietnamese to the bargaining table in the hope of finding a negotiated peace. McCain and the other POWs were ecstatic that the United States was bombing the North again. "We were fully aware that the only way we were ever going to get out was for our government to turn the screws on Vietnam," McCain writes.

Ironically, it was McCain's father, now head of naval operations in the Pacific, who dispatched the planes that flew once again over the skies of Hanoi. He knew his son could become a casualty.

By the fall of 1972, delegates on both sides were meeting in Paris to hammer out a way to end the war. Nixon suspended the bombing campaign. When talks broke down, the bombing resumed. On December 18, McCain and his fellow POWS at the Hanoi Hilton listened as American bombs dropped perilously close to the camp. It was the start of the so-called "Christmas Bombing." As the explosions echoed and rocked the camp, McCain and the other POWs cheered wildly. Nixon halted the bombing on December 30. A few days later, peace talks resumed.

Nearly a month later, on January 23, 1973, Nixon announced that the United States and the communists had reached an agreement to end American involvement in the war. This agreement included bringing McCain and the other POWs home.

Operation Homecoming began on February 12, 1973, when the first prisoners of war left Hanoi. Leading the contingent, among others, were Everett Alvarez, James Stockdale and Jeremiah Denton, who had spent the longest time in captivity.

American POWs are full of joy as they fly home to the United States in 1973. For many, the joy and relief of homecoming would be shortlived as they grappled with the effects of their imprisonment.

"Imagine you're imprisoned in a cage; imagine the cage surrounded by the smell of feces; imagine the rotted food you eat is so infested with insects that to eat only a few is a blessing; imagine knowing your life could be taken by one of your captors on a whim at any moment; imagine you are subjected to mental and physical torture designed to break not bones but instead spirit on a daily basis. That was being a prisoner of North Vietnam," wrote historian Andrew H. Lipps in his book *Operation Homecoming: The Return of American POWs from Vietnam.*

"Then imagine one day, after seemingly endless disappointment, you are given a change of clothes and lined up to watch an American plane land to return you home. That was Operation Homecoming."

McCain was in the third group of prisoners to leave. On March 14, he and a group of other POWs boarded an American plane that was waiting for them at the Gia Lam airport, just outside Hanoi. "I nearly cried at the sight of it," McCain writes in *Faith of My Fathers*. "At the airport, lined up in formation according to our shoot-down date, we maintained our military bearing as a noisy crowd of Vietnamese gawked at us.... When my name was called, I stepped forward..."

"We cheered loudly when the pilot announced that we were 'feet wet,' which meant that we were now flying over the Tonkin Gulf and in international air space," McCain writes. "A holiday atmosphere prevailed for the rest of the flight."

The former POWs ate sandwiches and enjoyed soft drinks. They joked. They told stories of their confinement, of the people they knew and the missions they had been on.

They talked so much, they could barely hear the wail of the plane's engines. The plane McCain was on headed to the Philippines. When Carol received the news, she gathered the kids inside their home outside Jacksonville, Florida, according to historian Timberg. "Your daddy is coming home," she said. "He is out. They cannot get him anymore." After five and a half years in captivity, John McCain was finally free.

CHAPTER 13

A New World

A PHOTOGRAPHER FOR THE ASSOCIATED PRESS was waiting patiently at Clark Air Base in the Philippines on March 14, 1973, as the Air Force C-141 carrying John McCain landed. As McCain hobbled down the plane's stairs, the photographer pointed the camera and captured on film a large smile across McCain's face. At the bottom of the ramp, Admiral Noel Gayler waited to shake hands with the former prisoner of war.

John McCain was once again front-page news. The photograph ran in the *New York Times* the following day with this caption: "ARRIVAL AT CLARK: Lieut. Cmdr. John S. McCain 3d limps from a plane at Clark Air Base."

More than 9,000 miles away in Jacksonville, McCain's family saw the image and wondered how their lives would change now that Johnny was home.

"Where will he sleep?" asked his six-year-old daughter Sidney, who was only a few months old when McCain shipped out to Vietnam.

"He will sleep in my bed, with me," Carol answered.

"And what will we feed him?" Sidney wanted to know.

The last time McCain had seen his family was in 1967, just before he shipped out on the *Oriskany*. So much had changed. Carol, as her mother-in-law did in World War II, had acted admirably as the family's field marshal, issuing orders, paying bills, blowing noses, comforting her children, going to soccer matches. All of that was about to change now that her husband was home, and Carol couldn't have been happier.

John McCain was determined to leave his experiences in Vietnam to the dust bin of history. "I have often maintained that I left Vietnam behind me when I arrived at Clark," McCain writes. "That is an exaggeration. But I did not want my experiences in Vietnam to [define] the rest of my life."

As for Carol, she was soon to come face to face with the horrors of Vietnam as never before.

To say Carol was excited to see her husband would have been an understatement. She looked forward to getting to know him again. She hoped their family would live happily ever after. But privately she was worried. She knew that time had changed all of them. The kids had grown, as had Carol. They were all different people. She hoped they would be able to recognize one another when John returned to them.

She knew her husband had been injured, but she didn't understand just how badly his body was broken. She needed to know what to expect when he arrived back in Florida.

To that end, the Navy sent a team of officers to the McCain house to brief Carol on her husband's injuries. They said her husband was physically not the same man he was in 1967. He was nearly crippled, they said. One of his legs was almost unworkable. He would need to undergo extensive physical therapy to unlock his frozen knee. His left arm was severely compromised. Further, McCain wanted to stay in the Navy as a pilot. But

John McCain waves to the public as he arrives at Jacksonville Naval Air Station in Florida on March 18, 1973, after spending five years as a POW. His wife and young son Doug (on crutches due to a soccer injury) are elated to see him.

the doctors said his injuries were too grave. McCain needed to understand that he would never pilot a jet fighter again.

A few days after arriving at Clark Air Base, McCain, walking with his new Navy-issue crutches, arrived in Jacksonville. As he stepped onto the runway in Jacksonville, he was embraced by his family. A smiling McCain wrapped his arms around his wife and children. His 14-year-old son, Doug was also on crutches. He had recently broken his leg in a soccer game. The newspapers wasted no time in chronicling the happy reunion. "No Limps of Joy in McCain Family Reunion" was the headline in Jacksonville's local paper the next day.

A Different Nation

The United States was different, too. The Vietnam War, along with civil unrest and the assassinations in 1968 of civil rights leader Dr. Martin Luther King Jr. and Senator Robert Kennedy, had taken its toll on the United States. While the POWs, McCain included, were welcomed home as warrior heroes, most Vietnam veterans were not. They felt the sting of scorn as the public tried to come to grips with the war and its aftermath. The anti-war protests that Hanoi Hannah had told the POWs about while they were in captivity had tossed the country into a political and social maelstrom. Things were not as they were when McCain took off from the *Oriskany* on that fateful day in October 1967.

Many people thought Vietnam was an unlawful war, a waste of money and life. The U.S. public had endured years of its government lying to them. By the end of the war, 58,000 Americans had died, and an untold number of North and South Vietnamese. The country was tired. Americans wanted to put Vietnam behind them as soon as possible.

John McCain III is reunited with his father, Admiral John S. McCain Jr., upon returning home to Jacksonville, Florida, from Vietnam in 1973.

At that time, Vietnam was the longest war fought in American history, a war the nation ultimately lost. Once the United States pulled out, the communists overran the South and created one nation just as Ho Chi Minh, the communist leader who had died in 1969, had wished.

"The Vietnam War was arguably the most traumatic experience for the United States in the 20th Century," wrote historian Donald M. Goldstein. "Now that is indeed a grim distinction in the span that included two world wars, the assassinations of two presidents and the resignation of another, the Great Depression, the Cold War, racial unrest, and the drug and crime waves."

For his part, McCain was the best-known prisoner of war and became an instant celebrity, a military rock star in a nation that had seemingly given up on heroes. He shook hands with President Nixon and, two months after stepping on U.S. soil for the first time in years, penned an article for the magazine *U.S. News & World Report*.

The story was massive by magazine standards, some 13 pages long. It was titled "Inside Story: How the POWs Fought Back." A reader might think that after being held captive and brutalized for five and a half years, McCain would be a bitter man. He wasn't. He was philosophical about his plight and accepted it in a way that would have made his grandfather proud. While McCain acknowledged that the country had changed in the years he had been away, he welcomed the new opportunities that it presented.

"Now that I'm back," he wrote, "I find a lot of hand-wringing about this country. I don't buy that. I think America today is a better country than the one I left nearly six years ago.... I think America is a better country now because we have been through a sort of purging process, a re-evaluation

President Richard M. Nixon thanks former POW John McCain
for his service at a meeting in Washington, D.C., in 1973.

of ourselves. Now I see more of an appreciation of our way of life. There is more patriotism. The flag is all over the place. I hear new values being stressed—the concern for environment is a case in point.

"I had a lot of time to think over there," McCain wrote at the end of the article, "and came to the conclusion that one of the most important things in life—along with a man's family—is to make some contribution to this country."

Copper Bracelets

After McCain returned home, he received dozens of letters from young men and women, many of whom had pledged support to American POWs. During the Vietnam War, many people wore a copper bracelet engraved with the name of a POW or soldier missing in action. The bracelets were the brainchild of a student group in California called Voices in Vital America. The project had its official kickoff on Veterans Day, November 11, 1970, when the group held a news conference. People around the country took notice and the group began receiving 12,000 requests a day for the bracelets. Families of these missing and imprisoned soldiers supported the project and the idea that the soldiers were remembered by the public back home.

Moving On

McCain began to reinvent himself after he arrived home, not only writing magazine articles but giving speeches and leading parades, which hundreds of people attended. He also began reading books about the policy decisions that had led to the war. He refused to apologize for his role in the conflict and was never hostile about his fate. "Nobody made me fly over Vietnam," he said on several occasions.

While he didn't agree with the anti-war protesters, he believed they were well within their rights as Americans to protest. He also understood those men who refused to fight. While many Vietnam veterans hated those who fled to Canada as "draft dodgers," McCain was more thoughtful and circumspect. He said those who evaded the draft are the only people who can judge themselves, acknowledging that he too had made mistakes in his life.

McCain spent nine months at the National War College in Fort McNair in Washington. During that period, he dealt with the long-term effects his experiences as a POW would likely have on his psyche. He learned to embrace the experience by using all that he had learned in captivity as a positive force. He wrote a paper on the Code of Conduct for prisoners. In it, McCain argued that the Code should be modified to represent more accurately the conditions prisoners of war might face. He said that if the enemy forces prisoners to make statements, the U.S. government should assume those statements were coerced through torture.

He also used the paper to give his own view of how the Vietnam War was conducted. McCain said the war itself was not wrong, but those in charge had not fought it correctly.

"I was not an embittered veteran before I entered the War College," McCain is quoted as saying in *John McCain: A Biography,* Elaine Povich's book on the Navy pilot. "But I did resent how badly civilian leaders had mismanaged the war and how ineffectually our senior military commanders had resisted their mistakes."

Specifically, McCain understood the racial and economic inequities in the draft, the process through which young men were required by law to serve in the military. He saw how the war was fought mainly by minorities, including African-Americans, and the poor, while the more affluent took advantage of "deferments," which allowed college students to sit out the war.

It was "appalling," McCain said, that "Americans had let the least fortunate among us fight the war for them while sons of privilege were afforded numerous opportunities to stay home. That was a political decision made not just by the president, Congress, and the services, but by the country as a whole and I resented the hell out of it."

The thesis provides a window into the views John McCain would hold as a politician—a transition that would soon come to pass. The time he spent educating himself on the run-up to the Vietnam War and its aftermath led to an understanding of how the United States conducted its foreign policy with other nations. "I learned a very important lesson that you cannot pursue a conflict that the American people will not support over time," Povich quotes McCain. "They will be patient, but over time they will not support foreign military operations that risk American lives unless you show them a path of success." This was just one of the guiding principles he adhered to as he became one of the decision makers affecting U.S. foreign policy.

McCain spent the next several years in the Navy, although he never flew again. He became restless and withdrew from his family. He began to believe his life had a different purpose.

McCain's marriage to Carol began to crumble. It wasn't a good time for either of them. McCain knew the war wasn't to blame for the deterioration of their relationship. Instead, it was his reaction to where he found himself after the years away. Eventually, Carol and John, who had both endured great pain during the war years, divorced.

Political Newcomer

The arrival of the 1980s brought tremendous change for John McCain. In 1980, at the age of 44, he married Cindy Lou Hensley, a 25-year-old graduate of the University of Southern California and a special education teacher. The couple had met one year earlier at a cocktail party and by all accounts fell instantly in love. Hensley had been raised in Phoenix, Arizona. She was the daughter of a wealthy family business owner who had strong ties to the state of Arizona and important connections with power brokers there. Those relationships would prove valuable to James Hensley's new son-in-law.

McCain courted Cindy by flying between Washington and Arizona to be with her. The two married six weeks after his divorce from Carol in April 1979.

Then on March 23, 1981, John McCain's father, John Sidney McCain Jr., son of "Slew" McCain, died. He had been in bad health, retiring from the Navy nine years before. The *New York Times* wrote, "Adm. John S. McCain Jr., a former commander in chief of Pacific forces in the Vietnam War and a World War II hero, died yesterday of a heart attack while on a military aircraft returning from Europe. He was 70 years old."

"I remember little of the five days between that moment and the morning we buried him at Arlington National Cemetery, among the rows of white headstones that mark the many thousands of carefully tended graves on its sloping green acres, not far from where his father lay," McCain writes in his book *Worth Fighting For*, which was published in 2002.

A few months before his dad died, McCain had told his father that he was leaving the Navy.

"My father's death and funeral occurred at a moment of great change for me and for the tradition that had brought honor to three generations of John McCains. I had arrived at my mother's apartment [for a reception after the funeral] still wearing my dress blue uniform. I would never wear it again. I left the reception after an hour or so and drove to an office in a nondescript building in Crystal City, Virginia.... There I signed my discharge papers.... For the first time in the twentieth century, and possibly forever, the name John McCain was missing from the Navy rosters."

At the time of his father's death, McCain was still in uniform, acting as the Navy's liaison officer to the United States Senate. His job was to lobby the Senate for things the Navy wanted. As the liaison officer, McCain says he became "intrigued by the enormous power over the nation's security" wielded by the members of the Senate's Armed Services Committee. He began meeting with some of the most powerful men in the nation and escorted many of them on overseas trips. He began to see a future for himself in politics, serving the people of the United States as a representative in their government.

The day his father was buried and John McCain quit the Navy, this son of admirals boarded a plane with his young wife, Cindy, for a new home in Phoenix, Arizona. It would be in the hot, dusty desert that John McCain, navy pilot, war hero, prisoner of war, would embark on a new chapter in his life, one that would take him, almost, to the pinnacle of power in the United States.

Upon arriving in Arizona, McCain became active in Republican Party politics. He traveled around the state introducing himself to Arizona's political elite, the men and women who held strings of power in the state. McCain did all the right things a political newcomer was supposed to do. He went to parades and Rotary Club and Kiwanis Club luncheons. He spoke about his biography, the war, and his plans for the future. "Hi, I'm John McCain," he said countless times, shaking countless hands. "I'm new to the state, and I'd like to come over and say hello."

His new father-in-law, Jim Hensley, hired his new son-in-law to work in his firm's public relations office. Hensley was one of the richest men in Arizona, and he made introductions that McCain used to forge relationships of his own. The job allowed McCain to travel around the state attending conventions and other gatherings promoting Hensley's business. Slowly, McCain began making contacts with people who could help him with his political aspirations. John McCain, however, was John McCain. That meant he was impatient. He wanted to get into politics now, today, not years from now. Politics is a subtle sport; a political career has to grow and mature. McCain wanted to be a candidate for office. But no openings existed.

That all changed in 1982 when Representative John Rhodes, a Republican, announced his retirement from Congress. McCain, who lived just outside Rhodes' district, was jubilant. He decided to move to the district, a short drive away, and run for the seat. Jay Smith, one of Arizona's leading Republican powerbrokers, did all he could to restrain McCain, who wanted to declare his candidacy immediately.

Smith told McCain to take a breath and slow down. He told McCain to build tension by first forming an "exploratory committee." This, Smith said, would cause the press to speculate, thus providing free publicity. McCain didn't like that strategy, but understood the value of Smith's experience. In late March, McCain announced his intention to seek the seat. By this time, three other candidates, all more experienced in politics than McCain, had entered the race for the Republican nomination. All had a good chance of winning. As for McCain, experts did not put much hope in his winning the nomination. However, if he did win in the solidly Republican district, it was as good as winning the general election.

McCain was a tireless campaigner. He went from door to door, shaking hands and asking people for their votes, not an easy thing to do in the sweltering summer heat in Phoenix where temperatures often reach more than 100 degrees. Still, McCain, with his boundless energy, knocked on doors in the district for six hours a day, six days a week. In the end, he visited 20,000 Republican houses and wore out three pairs of shoes.

Campaigning door-to-door can be difficult. Most people do not want to be bothered by strangers. "What are you selling?" was a question McCain often heard when he rapped on someone's door. No one really knew who John McCain was. Little by little, however, people began to recognize his face and his name.

McCain also worked to raise campaign funds. He produced television commercials that touted him as "a new leader for Arizona" and a man who "knows how Washington works." Some of the commercials pictured McCain with then President Ronald Reagan and his wife, Nancy. McCain had met the Reagans in 1973, just a few months after he returned home from the war. At the time of that meeting, Reagan was governor of California and a rising presence in the Republican Party. In other ads,

McCain was pictured standing near John Tower, a popular Republican senator from Texas. McCain also used his status as a veteran and POW to his advantage. People began asking for his autograph.

Election Day Jitters

Finally, primary day, the day on which the district's Republicans would go to the polls to vote for their congressional candidate, arrived. McCain's presence in the campaign office was distracting. He got in the way as his staff went about their tasks. He peppered them with questions and barked orders. Smith, seeing how crazy McCain was making everyone, told the candidate to take a hike, go somewhere else.

Reluctantly agreeing, McCain went to a movie—*Star Wars*. He couldn't sit still, however. He continually jumped up from his seat and paced the lobby floor. He went home and then to campaign headquarters as the votes were being tallied. He won with 32 percent of the vote. The general election later that year wasn't even close. McCain easily beat the Democratic candidate, William Hegarty.

"I came to a Congress in the middle of the 'Reagan Revolution.' No one had a more pronounced influence on my political convictions than Ronald Reagan," McCain writes. "I embraced all of the core Reagan convictions: faith in the individual; skepticism of government; free trade…a strong defense…. I thought the Reagan presidency was the best thing that had happened to America in a long time."

John McCain had made it to Washington. Privately, he had already begun to consider where he would go after his term in the House of Representatives ended.

CHAPTER 14

The Halls of Congress

In January 1983, Representative John McCain of Arizona again arrived in Washington, D.C., this time as a member of the House of Representatives. He was perceived by the press as a newly minted congressman who would serve as a reliable conservative vote for Ronald Reagan and his policies.

McCain idolized Reagan, a former actor turned politician. McCain supported Reagan's policies and saw that, as a leader and as a communicator, the president was trying to turn America around after years of war and political and government corruption. Reagan focused on strengthening the U.S. military and raged against communism and the Soviet Union.

In one way, the press was right about John McCain. He was indeed a reliable conservative Republican vote. He routinely clashed with the House's Democratic majority, much to the delight of the Reagan administration. But then came Lebanon. As a civil war upended that country and the United States was forced to involve itself, everything the media and political establishment believed about John McCain was thrown into disarray.

Breaking With the President

In 1975, a complicated civil war broke out between Muslims and Christians in Lebanon. By the early 1980s, Syria, Israel and the United Nations had tried to intervene in order to restore peace. At the time, Lebanon and other parts of the Middle East were unstable political entities, threatening to throw the region into further chaos.

In 1981, the nations of Syria and Israel backed different political factions in Lebanon. At the center of the conflict was Israel's most-hated enemy, the Palestine Liberation Organization (PLO). The PLO wanted to secure a homeland for Palestinians on land that was now part of Israel. The conflict between the two sides was threatening to engulf the entire region. The PLO routinely used Lebanon as a base to send missiles into northern Israel. The goal of American policymakers was to bring stability to Lebanon and figure out a way to prevent an all-out war between the PLO and Israel.

In August 1982, a multinational force, including U.S. Marines, arrived in Lebanon to keep the peace and oversee a negotiated Palestinian and Syrian withdrawal from the country. A cease-fire had been hammered out in the shadow of an American fleet that sailed offshore in the Mediterranean Sea.

Reagan wanted to keep the Marines in Lebanon for another 18 months, but needed the permission of Congress. While most Republicans agreed with the president, McCain did not. On September 28, 1983, the House of Representatives held a seven-hour debate on a resolution to invoke the War Powers Act, giving Reagan the authority to keep U.S. troops in Lebanon. The resolution had bipartisan support. If it passed, it would be the first time Congress invoked the War Powers Act, which it had approved after Vietnam as a way to limit the war-making powers of the president.

McCain, the freshman congressman, an unknown in the House of Representatives, rose to speak against the resolution. "The fundamental question is: What is the United States' interest in Lebanon?" he asked. "It is said we are there to keep the peace. I ask, what peace? It is said we are there to aid the government. I ask, what government? It is said we are there to stabilize the region. I ask, how can the U.S. presence stabilize the region?"

McCain was obviously thinking about the costly decisions that led the United States to intervene and stay in Vietnam. He didn't want the government to make the same mistake in Lebanon. "The longer we stay in Lebanon, the harder it will be for us to leave," he said. "We will be trapped by the case we make for having our troops there in the first place."

President Ronald Reagan meeting with John McCain at the White House.

McCain worried what U.S. allies would think if the Marines stayed in a land where they were not wanted. "We should consult with our allies and withdraw with them in concert if possible, unilaterally if necessary. I also recognize that our prestige may suffer in the short term, but I am more concerned with our long-term national interest."

Despite McCain's objections, the resolution passed overwhelmingly by a vote of 270 to 161. Nearly a month later, on October 23, 1983, a suicide bomber attacked the Marine headquarters in Beirut, killing 241 U.S. servicemen.

McCain's speech and vote against the resolution caught the eye of *Rolling Stone*, a liberal alternative magazine that rarely praised any Republican. "In the House of Representatives, a respected veteran of Vietnam…chose to remind his colleagues of that war's lessons," wrote William Greider. "It takes enormous courage for an older military man to deliver a message like that."

The vote was a watershed moment for the fledgling politician. It showed that McCain was not a rubber stamp for the administration's policies. Instead, he was willing to be an independent mind that was not afraid to go against the political grain even if it meant political and personal defeat.

A week after the Beirut bombing, the House voted on another resolution, this time to cut off money for the Marine deployment in Lebanon. Although McCain had not favored the deployment of U.S. troops in Lebanon, he was nevertheless realistic about supporting them there, as the destruction of the Marine barracks had changed the dynamic in the region.

"I voted against the resolution, which ultimately failed, because a withdrawal after the attack would instruct our enemies throughout the Middle East that they could win a conflict with the United States on the cheap—cheaply to them, anyway. I could not bring myself to help give [those] who had committed the atrocity the satisfaction of a full American retreat. It was a futile gesture."

Once again, McCain had bucked the system. In later years, he would wear his votes on Lebanon as a badge of honor. "In Lebanon, I stood up to President Reagan, my hero, and said, if we send Marines in there, how can we possibly, beneficially, affect this situation? Unfortunately, almost 300 brave young Marines were killed."

It wouldn't be the first time McCain would challenge the establishment, Democrat or Republican. His contrary stances on a number of issues earned him the moniker "maverick." A maverick is defined as an independent-minded person. In the eyes of many, John McCain was a person who followed his own heart and intellect no matter the political price.

Working for His Constituents

As a first-term congressman, McCain was attentive to his constituents back in Arizona. When Congress was in session, the workweek in Washington, D.C., ended on Thursday. When the day was over, McCain raced from the Capitol, where Congress met, to catch the last flight of the day back to Phoenix, a 4,000-mile trip. He wanted to make good on his campaign promise to return to his district every weekend.

Once he arrived home, McCain did not sit with his feet on the coffee table. Instead, he spent the weekend meeting with groups of people. He spoke to political and social clubs. He held town meetings. He shook hands and kept in touch with his voters, explaining his stance on particular issues. While he was in Washington, Cindy stayed in Arizona to cement the couple's ties to the district. It was a smart political move that paid off every election year.

On Sundays, McCain boarded a late-night flight out of Phoenix and returned to Washington so he could be in his office when work resumed on Monday. He was a tireless lawmaker. Moreover, he was a celebrity of sorts. Reporters flocked to his office and wrote admiring stories about him. He took a keen interest in foreign affairs and national security issues. He also took seats on congressional committees, such as those that handle water and land issues, which were important to the people of Arizona.

Despite some differences, McCain continued to be a stalwart supporter of the president. McCain used his first term in office wisely, building a political base that propelled him to a second term.

Back to Hanoi

A month after his re-election in 1984, CBS anchorman Walter Cronkite invited McCain to return to Hanoi with a film crew to mark the 10th anniversary of the end of the Vietnam War. The documentary was to air in April 1985. McCain agreed. It was a shrewd political move for a man who held higher aspirations. By returning to Vietnam, he would be able to tell his story to a new generation of Americans who might not remember all the details of the war or McCain's role in it.

Vietnam, now united under a communist government, remembered John McCain well and had little wish to revisit their relationship. At first, the Vietnamese government refused McCain a visa to enter the country. The admiral's son had been particularly irksome to the North Vietnamese, and they simply did not want to deal with him. In the end, the government relented and approved the visa. McCain, a film crew and Cronkite arrived in Hanoi in December and began filming.

John McCain, left, and Walter Cronkite, right, meet with local Vietnamese during the filming of a CBS news special in 1985.

CBS took McCain back to the area where he had been shot down and captured. A group of Vietnamese gathered around him, not knowing who the white-haired American was. They looked on as McCain and Cronkite visited a stone monument erected by the communists to celebrate the downing of McCain's airplane and his subsequent capture. The man on the statue had his head bowed and his arms outstretched to the sky. Cronkite told the onlookers that the man he was with, John McCain, was "the famous air pirate" identified on the monument's inscription. Suddenly, the crowd mobbed McCain. They shouted his name and vied to shake his hand. It was as if an old war hero had returned. Politics was nowhere to be seen as the man on the stone sculpture appeared before them.

McCain also visited the prison where he was held in Hanoi after the North Vietnamese captured him. "There was a great deal of pain here," he told Cronkite. "There was a great deal of suffering, a great deal of loneliness. There was also a lot of courage displayed."

On the night the documentary, "Honor, Duty, and a War Called Vietnam," aired, viewers saw Cronkite walking by the lake where McCain ended up in 1967 after his plane was blasted from the sky. "It has been almost eighteen years since former Navy pilot John McCain parachuted into that small Hanoi lake," Cronkite narrated. "Tonight, he will see it again, and the monument the Vietnamese built to commemorate his capture. He will also walk back into the cell where he spent much of his five and a half years as prisoner of war. Tonight, John McCain returns to his battlefield as we return to others in the war America did not win."

The *Arizona Republic* described McCain's appearance on the television special as "a true American hero returning to his prison camp." McCain felt the admiration and respect from people who came face to face with his past. The publicity it gave the would-be senator was invaluable. McCain began to think his dream of serving in the U.S. Senate might become a reality.

The Senate

Unlike the House of Representatives, where members serve for two-year terms, senators serve for six years before they are up for re-election. Because there are only 100 senators, compared to 435 House members, it is easier to compromise on legislation. The Senate often takes the long view on policy decisions.

Senator Barry Goldwater of Arizona would be retiring in 1987, when his term was up. Goldwater had been in the Senate for generations, first winning the seat in 1952. In his five terms, he never wavered from his stance as an ultraconservative politician. He ran for president against Lyndon Johnson in 1964, only to be humiliated on Election Day in a landslide.

With Goldwater retiring, McCain saw an opening. However, he had been in Congress only for a short while, and other, more seasoned Arizona political veterans were eyeing the seat. If McCain were to win the Republican nomination, experts expected he would have a tough fight in the general election. That's because people predicted the state's popular and young Democratic governor, Bruce Babbitt, would seek the Democratic nomination for the Senate seat.

McCain and his campaign staff looked at the political landscape and undertook an unusual and bold strategy. They planned to convince Babbitt, who people believed wanted to run for president one day, not to run for Goldwater's seat. From McCain's standpoint, if Babbitt lost the Senate race it would be political suicide. McCain felt a loss would doom any presidential ambitions Babbitt might harbor.

McCain's operatives tried various techniques to keep Babbitt from running. They made it known that McCain was going to run to win. McCain was raising a lot of money and barnstorming around the state. "No rural hamlet too remote to visit," Richard de Uriarte wrote about McCain in the *Phoenix Gazette*. "No fund-raiser he can't attend. No interest group he can't romance. No civic organization he can't address. No social event he won't grace with his Boy Scout earnestness. No constituent meeting he can't fit into his schedule."

Babbitt played the waiting game, refusing to commit. He saw in McCain an energetic and popular opponent—a war hero. On March 18, 1985, Babbitt put speculation to rest by announcing he was not going to run for the Senate in 1986. Denying that McCain had "bullied" him out of the race, Babbitt said his decision was the best for him and his family. "At this time in my life and our lives, it's not right for us," he said.

Still, McCain did not have a clear path to winning his party's nomination. A five-term congressman named Bob Stump stood in his way. "Bob and I weren't adversaries, but we weren't the best of friends, either," McCain writes. "I'm sure he thought me undeserving of the nomination because my ties to Arizona and my political experience were shallow compared to his. He had the unofficial but active support of Barry Goldwater's chief aide, Judy Eisenhower, who for reasons unknown to me didn't care for me one bit."

McCain also faced another, formidable hurdle—Barry Goldwater. McCain wanted the outgoing senator's endorsement. "I really don't think he liked me much," McCain writes. "I don't know why that was.... I always showed him great deference. Every several months, I would ask for an appointment to see him.... We never disagreed or quarreled. I wanted to succeed him, so of course there was an element of courtesy to him. But that was a small part of it.... I wanted him to like me."

As it turned out, McCain didn't have to worry about Stump or Goldwater. Stump decided to seek another term in the House. McCain became the Republican candidate and went on to beat his Democratic challenger, Richard Kimball, in the 1986 general election. John McCain was now where he wanted to be.

Trouble for the President

John McCain was an incoming U.S. senator and his hero, Ronald Reagan, was in trouble. A scandal, the Iran-Contra affair, was threatening Reagan's second term. The scandal had its roots in the lush, verdant jungles of Nicaragua, a country in Central America. It was there that an anti-communist group called the Contras was battling the Sandinistas, a leftist organization backed by communist Cuba.

Reagan described the Contras as freedom fighters, "the moral equivalent of our Founding Fathers." Reagan was an ardent anti-communist. His administration, specifically the Central Intelligence Agency, assisted anti-communist groups such as the Contras. In 1984, however, Congress passed a law that made financially supporting the Contras nearly impossible. Despite the law, the president told his national security adviser, Robert McFarlane, "to do whatever you can to help these people keep body and soul together."

In 1985, Iran and Iraq were at war. Five years before, Iraq had invaded Iran, fearing civil unrest in that country would spread across the border to its own domain. Iraq also wanted to become a dominant state in the

Persian Gulf region, and control of Iran would be vital to that goal. Iran needed weapons to fight Iraq and wanted to buy them from the United States. Congress, however, had passed a law making it illegal to sell arms to Iran, which in 1979 had held 52 American diplomats and citizens hostage for 444 days. McFarlane went to the president and sought his advice, advocating a number of reasons why the sale should go through.

Reagan listened, with another agenda on his mind. Seven American hostages were being held by Iranian terrorists in Lebanon. Could the United States sell arms to Iran in exchange for the release of the hostages? Many in the Reagan White House opposed the deal. Despite the arms embargo, however, the United States secretly began selling Iran weapons. When the story broke in a Lebanese newspaper in 1986, Reagan denied any such deal. A week later he went on television to explain the deal to the public, retracting his earlier denial.

A subsequent investigation by the U.S. attorney general found that only $12 million of the $30 million the Iranians reportedly paid for the weapons had been sent to the U.S. Treasury. The remainder of the money, it turned out, had been funneled to the Contras. Vice Admiral John Poindexter, head of the National Security Council, was one of the key players implicated in the scandal—the very same John Poindexter who had been McCain's classmate at the Naval Academy. The tables had turned on the Annapolis rabble-rouser and his old friend Poindexter, who had been first in their class and a model student.

Poindexter soon resigned. McCain, not yet sworn in as a senator, was still a member of the House Armed Services Committee, which began holding hearings on the matter. He had heard that his old friend Poindexter was going to plead the Fifth Amendment when he testified before the committee. The Fifth Amendment protected Poindexter from implicating himself in a crime.

McCain tried to persuade Poindexter not to plead the Fifth. McCain thought it was wrong that a Navy admiral should hide behind the U.S. Constitution. "John, you can't do it," McCain pleaded. When their meeting broke up, Poindexter walked from McCain's office into the committee room where he refused to answer a question on the grounds that it might incriminate himself.

Several months later Poindexter testified that he did not inform the president of his decision to shuttle money to the Contras. When NBC reporter Tom Brokaw asked McCain about Poindexter's claim that he did not tell the president about diverting the money from the Iranian weapons sale to the Contras, McCain was aghast. "I know John to be a man of the highest integrity," McCain said. "At the same time, it is difficult to comprehend why he would not inform the President of activities of that magnitude.... I think he made a terrible mistake."

McCain's comments angered many in his own party, especially supporters of Poindexter. It was another indication that McCain, despite politics, was going to speak his own mind.

Weathering the Storm

On October 8, 1989, the *Arizona Republic* published a story that tied McCain to a man named Charles Keating, a campaign donor who was at the center of a financial scandal known as the U.S. Savings and Loan crisis during the late 1980s.

John McCain in a Los Angeles courtroom during the trial of Charles Keating in 1991.

Although innocent of any crime, McCain, along with five other senators, were ensnared in the scandal. McCain and the others were investigated for helping the financier and donor. For the next three years, the scandal threatened McCain's political future. His re-election campaign was on the horizon. Would he run or not? He told aides that it was the worst thing to happen to him in his life.

Yet McCain was able to weather the storm. Although the Senate Ethics Committee reprimanded him for his connection to Keating, it cleared McCain of any wrongdoing. McCain won re-election and learned a very important lesson. From then on, "I carefully avoided situations that might even tangentially be construed as a less than proper use of my office," McCain writes. "I have refrained from intervening with regulators or supporting legislation or advocating anything for any purpose that doesn't serve an obvious public interest and that isn't in accord with my general governing philosophy."

McCain Takes Control

With the scandal behind him, McCain once again became fully enmeshed in the business of the Senate. He led the battle in 1989 to get an old friend, John Tower, confirmed as U.S. Secretary of Defense. Although McCain lost this fight, the bruising battle earned him respect among his Senate colleagues.

In 1989, McCain won a major legislative victory by forcing the repeal of a health insurance law that he believed would hurt many people. In victory, McCain defied Republican as well as Democratic leaders who supported the measure.

As the years rolled on, McCain solidified his reputation as a maverick. In 2000, he defied the Republican hierarchy and opposed tax cuts for the rich. While other Republicans denied the existence of and damage caused by climate change, McCain understood and accepted the science. In 2008, he visited a wind power plant in Oregon and told onlookers, "Instead of idly debating the precise extent of global warming or the precise timeline of global warming, we need to deal with the central facts of rising temperatures, rising waters and all the endless troubles that global warming will bring. We stand warned by serious and credible scientists across the world that time is short and the dangers are great.... I will not shirk the mantle of leadership that the United States bears."

McCain championed campaign finance reform. In 2002, he, along with Senator Russ Feingold, fought for and passed the McCain-Feingold Act, which banned a key source of funding for both parties—"soft money." Soft money is a donation to a political party that people can give for "party-building" activities, such as getting voters to the polls on Election Day. Although such contributions were not supposed to be used to support the candidacy of a particular president, congressman or senator, people could give as much as they wanted. Such donations were loosely regulated by the Federal Election Commission.

McCain-Feingold changed all that. It stipulated that all donations to national candidates or parties must come in the form of "hard money," which is subject to contribution limits and tight restrictions.

Over the years, John McCain became a lion of the Senate. There was one more place he wanted to be, however—1600 Pennsylvania Avenue, the White House.

CHAPTER 15

Fight for the Presidency

JOHN McCAIN'S GRANDFATHER AND FATHER had storied careers. They had served their country with distinction, put their lives on the line, and tried to do what was best for family and country. While John McCain III also did those things, he wanted something more. He entered politics, first becoming a congressman and then a respected senator. Thirteen years after first entering Congress, he did something his father and grandfather had probably not imagined for themselves. In 1999, McCain announced he was seeking the Republican presidential nomination.

The road to that decision had begun in 1996, when McCain was included on a short list of possible vice-presidential candidates. At that time, a Republican senator, Robert Dole, was running against President Bill Clinton. Dole ended up picking former Congressman Jack Kemp to be on his ticket. Dole lost the election to the Democrat, but McCain, in one political way, won. That year, *Time* magazine named McCain as one of the "25 Most Influential People in America." He was one of the brightest stars in the Republican Party.

On September 27, 2000, McCain stood before a crowd in Nashua, New Hampshire, site of the first Republican primary, and declared his intention to be the next president of the United States. He was running, he said, because "I owe America more than she has ever owed me."

Uphill Climb

Winning the Republican nomination was not going to be easy, and McCain knew this. The governor of Texas, George W. Bush, son of former President George H.W. Bush, was leading in the polls of prospective Republican voters. The Bush family was a political dynasty, a juggernaut that could raise enormous amounts of cash, something McCain could not do. The former President Bush had a bevy of supporters and advisers who would be more than happy to help his son win the nomination.

As for McCain, he was unsure whether Republican voters would embrace his candidacy. "I didn't believe I had the best shot, but I believed I had a shot," McCain would later write. "I was convinced I wouldn't ever become afraid of losing, a pretty easy virtue when you're an underdog. I expected to take courage from my fatalism to keep my campaign honest and original, if at times, a little less disciplined than necessary. I played the happy insurgent, with a zest for challenging authority and political conventions."

Although he had served in the Senate for nearly two decades, McCain was sure most Americans didn't know who he was. Polls of likely Republican primary voters showed that 50 percent knew who he was, which meant 50 percent did not. Less than 10 percent said they would vote for him.

Undeterred, McCain traveled from state to state telling Republican voters what he stood for. McCain beat Bush in New Hampshire, the first primary of the season. As a result, the once civil discourse between the campaigns began to fade. Bush's attacks on McCain grew more fierce, especially in the all-important South Carolina primary. Bush bested McCain in South Carolina and ended up winning the Republican nomination. Many political insiders believe that had McCain won the South Carolina primary he might have won the GOP nomination.

George W. Bush went on to defeat Vice President Al Gore in a controversial contest in which Bush won the Electoral College vote, but lost the popular vote.

McCain, beaten and bruised, went back to the Senate. He continued his independent streak, battling President Bush on a number of issues. It didn't matter that both were from the same party. Yet the White House remained on McCain's mind.

The Run for President: 2008

By 2006, McCain was again making plans to seek his party's nomination for president. George W. Bush was in the middle of his second and final term, and in the eyes of many, McCain was the front-runner in a field of nearly a dozen Republican presidential hopefuls. When the clock chimed noon on a damp and chilly April 26, 2007, McCain stood before a small crowd of supporters at a park in Portsmouth, New Hampshire, a year and a half before Election Day, and officially announced his candidacy.

"We've begun another campaign season earlier than many Americans prefer," McCain said. "So soon after our last contentious election, our differences are again sure to be sharpened and exaggerated. That's the nature of free elections. But even in the heat of a campaign, we shouldn't lose sight that much more defines us than our partisanship; much more unites us than divides us. We have common purposes and common challenges, and we live in momentous times. This election should be about big things, not small ones."

Senator McCain greeting supporters at a rally marking his 100th Town Hall Meeting in January 2008 in New Hampshire.

Eleven other Republicans were running, including Texas congressman Ron Paul, former Massachusetts governor Mitt Romney, and former Arkansas governor Mike Huckabee. When the primary season with its speeches, rallies and debates ended, McCain handily won the required number of GOP delegates. His Democratic opponent in 2008 would be first-term senator Barack Obama, the first African-American to run for president on a major party ticket.

Although they represented two different parties, McCain and Obama were a lot alike. They both argued that nothing could get done in Washington, D.C., because the government, they said, was locked in partisan gridlock and run by special interest groups that did not care about the people. Each said he could fix the system and bring a new era of cooperation to government.

A Struggling Campaign

Almost from the beginning, McCain's campaign sputtered. Early in the race, some 67 percent of Americans said they liked McCain. He was even in the polls with Obama, the senator from Illinois, in a head-to-head matchup. As the campaign season wore on, however, Obama, who had less experience in government than McCain, seemed to grow more popular by the day.

Obama had a lot of charisma, and the historic nature of his run was a high hurdle for McCain to leap. Obama was also funny. He was a talented orator and drew people in with his inspiring speeches. The younger senator became something of a celebrity, like a rock star of sorts in the world of politics, much as McCain had been when he came home from Vietnam.

Meanwhile, the Arizona senator's campaign was not catching on with the public. Americans were unclear about his platform. He thought the press was going easy on Obama, refusing to challenge the senator with tough questions. Obama, McCain said, was a newcomer to Washington and did not have the political scars that McCain had earned.

Despite McCain's misgivings, however, Obama was beating him in the polls. McCain asked Steve Schmidt, a political consultant from California, to right the campaign's floundering ship.

Schmidt came on board and didn't like what he saw. He was blunt with the old war veteran. Things weren't going well, he told McCain, not at all. Was he willing to do what it took?

McCain said yes, then pleaded with Schmidt: "Will you help me?"

Schmidt said he would, because there was nothing to lose. Be yourself, Schmidt told McCain, and people will respond.

With his political life on the line, McCain put Schmidt in charge, and the balding, burly political adviser slowly turned things around. Schmidt restored order. The campaign, and McCain himself, became more disciplined. Workers now knew what to do. While McCain loved talking to reporters on a variety of subjects, Schmidt limited the press's access to McCain to stop him from saying anything that deviated from their agreed-upon script for each issue.

With Schmidt's discipline, McCain began to have more fun on the campaign trail. He joked and became more confident. Still, despite his years serving his country as a warrior and a public servant, it was hard for McCain to find a chink in Obama's armor. By the summer of 2008, Obama was up an average of nearly seven points.

In July, Obama improved his image further by traveling to Europe and the Middle East, visiting eight countries in 10 days. The tour made Obama look presidential and diplomatic—someone who could be trusted on the world stage. In Berlin, 200,000 enthusiastic fans attended a speech by Obama. Images of the crowd cheering and clapping were beamed around the world.

McCain had no choice but to attack Obama's tour. McCain announced his campaign slogan, "Country First." The insinuation was clear: that Barack Obama—personable, funny, articulate—was cultivating his own celebrity instead of caring about the nation. Still, this and other attacks did not move the needle one bit for McCain. The public still seemed underwhelmed by McCain. Whereas Obama drew huge, enthusiastic crowds, the nation seemed unimpressed with the Arizona senator. The Republican and Democratic conventions were close, and Obama was ahead in every poll.

"We're running against the biggest celebrity in the world," Schmidt is quoted as saying in *Game Change* by John Heilemann and Mark Halperin.

McCain and his advisers decided to use Obama's celebrity against him. McCain likened the senator from Illinois to the celebrities Britney Spears and Paris Hilton. The campaign even put out advertisements using images of Obama, Spears and Hilton. "He's the biggest celebrity in the world," one ad said, "but is he ready to lead?"

A Bold Move

McCain was in deep trouble. He and his campaign manager knew they needed to shake up the race. But how? Obama had beat, among others, Senator Hillary Clinton in the Democratic primaries. Perhaps the time had come to put a woman on the ticket. Voters might look at that decision as a "maverick" move, the kind that had made McCain famous.

Republican presidential candidate John McCain speaks
to a crowd in Columbus, Ohio, during his 2008 campaign.

"The plan was always for McCain to shock the world with his vice-presidential pick," Heilemann and Halperin write. "For weeks his top advisors had been dreaming and scheming, touching bases and laying groundwork, secretly readying an announcement at once unconventional, unexpected, and unprecedented, which would throw the press and both parties for a loop and redraw the map.... McCain's VP choice had to be a game changer."

As a result, McCain agreed to pick Sarah Palin, the virtually unknown governor of Alaska, as his vice-presidential running mate. It was a bold move. A risky move. A move that underscored McCain's maverick behavior throughout his life.

The move baffled President Bush, who saw the choice of Palin announced on television in the White House. Vice President Dick Cheney had his own opinion. He told his friends that McCain had made a "reckless choice."

Only time would tell.

Falling Short

At first, McCain's pick of 44-year-old Sarah Palin seemed to give the senator's campaign the energy it needed. "She had attended five colleges, and had been a beauty queen, a sportscaster, and the two-term Mayor of Wasilla, a tiny town where she lived with her snowmobiling husband, Todd, and five children," Heilemann and Halperin write. Her politics were conservative, which made the Republican base happy.

Her electrifying speech at the Republican National Convention in early September seemed to be just what the campaign needed. For a while it was. Donations spiked. More and more volunteers signed up to canvass door to door in hopes of persuading voters to vote for John McCain. The race tightened dramatically. One poll had McCain up by 10 points as the election season moved into full swing.

Despite these early signs of hope, however, McCain's pick of Palin turned out to be a political mistake. The provincial Alaska governor could not, or would not, grasp simple policy issues. One famous example came when Palin, who had no foreign policy experience, told a journalist that she had some "insight" into Russia. "They are our next-door neighbors, and you can actually see Russia from land here in Alaska," she said. The naive comment shocked most politicians and made Palin a caricature on late-night TV.

Senator John McCain with Sarah Palin, his choice for his vice-presidential running mate in the 2008 election.

Things only got worse from there. Palin's style had seemed to be just what McCain's advisers thought his campaign needed. But Palin lacked the knowledge of history and global affairs to back it up. She also lacked the patience and wherewithal to study the material and drill until the information was second nature to her; the substance needed to match the style fell frighteningly short.

Character and Integrity

By the end of September, the McCain campaign was back in crisis mode. Obama had again overtaken McCain in the polls. In addition to Palin's missteps, the economy was imploding and the country found itself in the grip of a deep financial crisis. As banks and investment houses failed and people lost their jobs and homes, McCain insisted that "the fundamentals of the economy are sound." For many, McCain's comment showed he was out of touch with what was happening in America.

Still, there were times during the campaign when all the things McCain had learned throughout his life, all the hardships he endured, all the rules his grandfather, father, and mother taught him, shone brightly through. McCain's character and integrity were on display for all to see during one campaign rally when a woman came up to McCain and said, "I can't trust Obama. I have read about him, and…he's an Arab."

The woman's comment articulated the prejudice many felt about Barack Obama at that time. He had an unusual-sounding name and his father was born in Kenya, a country in Africa. Conspiracies about where Obama himself was born dogged the senator. Racial prejudice played a role in the election. Many people didn't want to see an African-American in the White House.

The woman's question sparked a response in McCain that showed his true character. He took the microphone from the woman and lectured her. "No, ma'am," McCain said. "He's a decent family man, a citizen that I just happen to have disagreements with on fundamental issues, and that's what this campaign is all about."

His comment shocked McCain's loyal audience and defied political convention. He knew he would anger some of his supporters, but didn't care. He continued to defend Obama. "He's a decent person and a person that you do not have to be scared of," he said. "If I didn't think I'd be one heck of a better President I wouldn't be running, and that's the point. I admire Senator Obama and his accomplishments. I will respect him. I want everyone to be respectful, and let's make sure we are. Because that's the way politics should be conducted in America."

Election Lost

In the end, McCain lost the election. He wasn't bitter. He knew that in every presidential contest, there is a winner and a loser. He had come out on the short end, but he still had a role to play. Politics is politics, after all. He had to make a concession speech on the night he lost the presidency. Such speeches are not about whether the losers accept their loss, but about uniting the loser's supporters behind the president-elect.

That's exactly what McCain did. He stood in front of his supporters and gave perhaps the best conciliatory speech in this nation's history. It was the end of a long and difficult struggle to win the the highest office in the land.

McCain knew Obama's win as the first African-American president was historic. It meant a lot of things to a lot of people, especially those who were treated like second-class citizens because of the color of their skin. Although McCain had criticized Obama during the campaign as inexperienced, the Arizona senator now got up in front of his supporters and said, "in a contest as long and as difficult as this campaign has been, his success alone commands my respect for his ability and perseverance.

Senator John McCain, flanked by his wife, Cindy, and his running mate, Sarah Palin, with her husband, Todd, delivers a concession speech to the nation upon his loss to Barack Obama in 2008.

"But that he managed to do so by inspiring the hopes of so many millions of Americans who had once wrongly believed that they had little at stake or little influence in the election of an American president is something I deeply admire and commend him for achieving. This is an historic election, and I recognize the special significance it has for African-Americans and for the special pride that must be theirs tonight."

McCain then told that crowd that he and Obama "both recognize that though we have come a long way from the old injustices that once stained our nation's reputation and denied some Americans the full blessings of American citizenship, the memory of them still had the power to wound.

"America today is a world away from the cruel and prideful bigotry of that time. There is no better evidence of this than the election of an African-American to the presidency of the United States. Let there be no reason now for any American to fail to cherish their citizenship in this, the greatest nation on Earth."

The speech was classic John McCain. He was always a fighter, a survivor, gracious in victory, courteous in defeat. The speech was a profile in courage. It brought tears to the eyes of both his supporters and his detractors.

CHAPTER 16

The Maverick's Toughest Battle

AFTER HIS LOSS IN 2008, John McCain returned to the Senate where he planned to finish out his years in office and his career. Neither he nor the savviest political observers would have imagined that eight years later he would be back in the presidential spotlight.

In 2015, New York businessman and reality TV star Donald J. Trump announced he was seeking the Republican presidential nomination. Most people did not believe Trump was a serious candidate, especially after he made disparaging remarks about various ethnic groups. When reporters asked McCain what he thought about some of Trump's comments, the senator was critical.

McCain disagreed with the way Trump ran his campaign. Talking about an America that was in decline went against everything that McCain had stood for personally, professionally and especially as a military man. Although both men were Republicans, McCain never hesitated to censure Trump whenever the senator thought Trump was wrong.

Calling Out the President

Trump eventually won the Republican nomination and the general election, becoming president of the United States. McCain voted with Trump's position 90.5 percent of the time, but that was still considered a very low number for a senator who was aligned with the same party as the president.

McCain's actions proved that he was still a maverick, and not even the president of the United States, no matter the party, could rob him of that designation. McCain first defied Reagan, then Bush, then Obama, and now the newest occupant of the office.

The most poignant example of McCain's independence came with the flair and zeal he had been noted for throughout his life. McCain was asked to vote on a Republican measure to repeal the health insurance law called the Affordable Care Act, one of President Obama's signature achievements and one that Trump wanted to do away with. The majority of Republican senators supported Trump's position.

After studying the measure to repeal the law, McCain voted "no" on the measure, literally giving the thumbs-down signal when he voted. He voted against the bill not because he wanted to defy the president, but because he didn't like the way the bill had been pushed through Congress without enough debate and because he was unsure how much the measure would cost.

"I cannot in good conscience vote for the...proposal," McCain said at the time. "I believe we could do better working together, Republicans and Democrats, and have not really tried. Nor could I support it without knowing how much it will cost, how it will affect insurance premiums, and how many people will be helped or hurt by it." This vote and others further cemented McCain's reputation as a politician who followed his own heart and mind in order to do what he thought best for all Americans.

The senator had fought many battles, personal and political, in his lifetime. Many times, he had come out on top. But in July 2017, John McCain announced he was fighting the greatest foe of them all—a lethal form of brain cancer. Doctors told the senator he had a 3 to 14 percent chance of surviving the illness. All his life he had played the cards he was dealt. The cancer diagnosis was just another hand he was playing.

After his diagnosis, McCain returned to the U.S. Senate amid cheers of adulation from his colleagues. He then gave what some consider one of the greatest speeches of his life. He wanted lawmakers from both parties to work together to get things done for the American people.

"Our responsibilities are important, vitally important, to the continued success of our Republic," he said.

In the long history of the United States, only a handful of people have accomplished what John McCain has accomplished, whether as a warrior, a statesman or a lawmaker. Even he would admit that yes, he was feisty. Yes, he was rowdy. Yes, he was brusque and temperamental. He spoke his mind perhaps too much. But he did it because of an undying love for his country.

In the world of national politics, McCain will always be regarded as one of the giants of the U.S. Senate, a politician who was not afraid to thumb his nose at the prevailing political winds. During his public life, he has done more for his country than most U.S. presidents can hope to achieve during their stay in office.

"All lives are a struggle against selfishness," he wrote in *Worth Fighting For*. "All my life I've stood a little apart from the institutions I willingly joined. It just felt natural to me. But in a life that shared no common purpose, my maverick nature, if that is what it truly is, wouldn't have amounted to much beyond eccentricity."

A lion in politics and a hero in war, McCain was admittedly high-strung and a boisterous malcontent. In short, he was human. But unlike most people, McCain was able to temper those emotions with loyalty and service to his country. That's because the memory of his grandfather and father, who instilled in him the values of loyalty and service, was his constant companion.

Senator McCain is embraced by Senate Minority Leader Charles Schumer of New York as McCain arrives on the Senate floor in July 2017.

McCain readily admitted he was ambitious, driven by personal success, public acclaim, and an overriding ambition to lead. "But only when I have joined my interests to my country's have politics been personally satisfying to me. I find no lasting satisfaction or honor in any virtue I admire, honesty or courage or independence, if I possess them only to flatter my own vanity."

John McCain viewed politics, often described as a blood sport, as a personal battlefield. But as one critic remarked, politics is extremely "personal for McCain. It is all a matter of honor and integrity."

McCain himself writes, "There is no honor or happiness in just being strong enough to be left alone.... I've had a good long run.... I could leave now satisfied that I have accomplished enough things that I believe are useful to the country to compensate for the disappointment of my mistakes.... My time might be passing.... I might yet become the man I always wanted to be."

When John McCain announced that he had been diagnosed with brain cancer in September 2017, it was a shock for many who had thought the senator invincible. "I've been through worse," he told a colleague.

Hero, fighter, survivor. It's impossible not to use such clichés when painting a portrait of John McCain. Yes, John McCain has an outsized ego, and yes, he dreams big, often to his own detriment. Yet he has always had the grit to make his life mean something. And that, it can be argued, is John McCain's greatest legacy.

Sources

American Presidency Project. "John McCain."http://www.presidency.ucsb.edu/ws/index.php?pid=76560

Apple, R.W. "Adm. McCain's Son, Forrestal Survivor, Is Missing in Raid." *New York Times*. October 28, 1967.

———. "At Least 70 Dead in Forrestal Fire; 89 Others Missing." *New York Times*. July 30, 1967.

Archive.org. "Full Text of John McCain Vietnam War POW CIA—Department of Defense Files." https://archive.org/stream/JohnMccainVietnamWarPowCia-DepartmentOfDefenseFiles/JohnMccainCiaFiles_djvu.txt

Bender, Bryan. "A Pilot's Sacrifice Helped Defuse Cuban Missile Crisis." *Boston Globe*. October 27, 2012.

CNN.com. "Transcript: McCain Concedes Presidency." November 5, 2008. http://edition.cnn.com/2008/POLITICS/11/04/mccain.transcript/index.html

Congressional Medal of Honor Society. George E. Day. http://www.cmohs.org/recipient-detail/3257/day-george-e.php

Diaz, Daniella. "McCain on His Cancer Prognosis. It's 'Very, Very, Serious.'" CNN. September 25, 2017. https://www.cnn.com/2017/09/25/politics/john-mccain-cancer-trump-health-care-60-minutes/index.html

Farley, Robert. "Was McCain Born in the USA?" Politifact.com. May 12, 2008. http://www.politifact.com/truth-o-meter/article/2008/may/12/born-usa/

Hawk, Amy. *Six Years in the Hanoi Hilton: An Extraordinary Story of Courage and Survival in Vietnam*. Washington, D.C.: Regnery Publishing. 2017.

Heilemann, John, and Mark Halperin. *Game Change*. New York: Harper Collins. 2010.

History.com. "This Day in History." http://www.history.com/this-day-in-history/johnson-approves-operation-rolling-thunder

History.net. "Interview—Everett Alvarez—A Vietnam POW for the Duration." April 11, 2013. http://www.historynet.com/interview-everett-alvarez-a-vietnam-pow-for-the-duration.htm

Journal of Applied Social Psychology. "Coping Activities in Solitary Confinement of U.S. Navy POWS in Vietnam." September, 1977.

Kaplan, Thomas, and Robert Pear. "McCain Announces Opposition to Republican Health Bill, Likely Dooming It." *New York Times*. September 22, 2017.

McCain Institute. "Cindy McCain." https://www.mccaininstitute.org/staff/cindy-mccain/

McCain, John. *Faith of Our Fathers*. New York: Random House. 1999.

———. "John McCain, Prisoner of War: A First-Person Account." *U.S. News & World Report*.

———. *Worth Fighting For*. New York: Random House. 2002.

National Archives. Executive Orders: Executive Order 10631—Code of Conduct for Members of the Armed Forces of the United States. https://www.archives.gov/federal-register/codification/executive-order/10631.html

National Museum of American History. "POW Bracelets." http://americanhistory.si.edu/collections/search/object/nmah_1273063

New York Times. "Admiral J.S. McCain Dies on Coast at 61." September 7, 1945.

New York Times. "Adm. John S. McCain Jr. Is Dead; Ex-Commander of Pacific Forces." March 24, 1981.

New York Times. "McCain Promotion Approved." September 4, 1949.

New York Times. "McCain's Speech of Climate Change." May 12, 2008.

Nowicki, Dan. "Here's a Blow-by-Blow Account of the Donald Trump vs. John McCain Feud." *Arizona Republic*. October 15, 2016.

O'Brien, Jane. "The POW Who Built a Multi-Million Dollar Business." BBC News. September, 2014. http://www.bbc.com/news/business-29027464

PBS. "The Iran-Contra Affair." http://www.pbs.org/wgbh/americanexperience/features/reagan-iran/

Povich, Elaine S. *John McCain: A Biography*. Westport, CT: Greenwood Press. 2009.

Segarra, Lisa Marie. "Watch John McCain Strongly Defend Barack Obama During the 2008 Campaign." Time.com. http://time.com/4866404/john-mccain-barack-obama-arab-cancer/

Sterba, James P. "P.O.W. Commander Among 108 Freed." *New York Times*. March 15, 1973.

Timberg, Robert. *John McCain: An American Odyssey*. New York: Free Press. 1999.

———. *The Nightingale's Song*. New York: Touchstone. 1995.

U.S. Naval Academy. A Brief History of USNA. https://www.usna.edu/USNAHistory/

———. Honor Concept. https://www.usna.edu/About/honorconcept.php

———. Qualifications of a Naval Officer. https://www.usna.edu/StrategicPlan/naval_officer_quals.php

Vasey, Joan B. "Veterans, Community Come Together for Vietnam War 50th Anniversary Commemoration." October 9, 2015. https://www.army.mil/article/156937/veterans_community_come_together_for_vietnam_war_50th_anniversary_commemoration

Wikipedia. "Keating Five." https://en.wikipedia.org/wiki/Keating_Five

Image Credits

Alamy
Bob Daemmrich: 102; dpa picture alliance: 14; Everett Collection: 53, 76; PJF Military Collection: 9

Associated Press
18, 58, 81, 136, 138, 162; © C-SPAN2: 182; © Horst Faas: 113, 126; © Harvey Georges: 140; © Jacquelyn Martin: 3; © Kiichiro Sato: 172

Getty Images
© Terry Ashe/The LIFE Images Collection: 7, 21; © Bettmann: 31; © Jon Brenneis/The LIFE Picture Collection: 116; © CBS Photo Archive: 155; © Darren Hauck: 174; © Andrew Harrer/Bloomberg: 177; © Derek Hudson: 107; © David Hume Kennerly: 97, 168; © Win McNamee: 4

Library of Congress
Carol M. Highsmith: 151

National Archives
Department of Defense: 131

Seth Poppel/Yearbook Library
25, 27

U.S. Air Force
68, 73, 83, 88

U.S. Navy
43, 47, 64

Index

Index

Index

Index